THE ENVIRONMENT

THE ENVIRONMENT: ITS ROLE IN PSYCHOSOCIAL FUNCTIONING AND PSYCHOTHERAPY

CAROLYN SAARI

COLUMBIA UNIVERSITY PRESS / NEW YORK

COLUMBIA UNIVERSITY PRESS
Publishers Since 1893
New York   Chichester, West Sussex

Library of Congress Cataloging-in-Publication Data
Saari, Carolyn.
The environment : its role in psychosocial functioning and psychotherapy /
Carolyn Saari.
p. cm.
Includes bibliographical references (p.) and indexes.
ISBN 0-231-12196-2 (cloth : alk. paper)
ISBN 0-231-12197-0 (pbk. : alk. paper)
1. Environmental psychology. 2. Social psychology.   I. Title.

BF353.S27 2002
155.9—dc21   2001047447
∞

Columbia University Press books are printed
on permanent and durable acid-free paper.
Printed in the United States of America
Designed by Lisa Hamm
c 10 9 8 7 6 5 4 3 2 1
p 10 9 8 7 6 5 4 3 2 1

CONTENTS

ACKNOWLEDGMENTS

S INCE THE IDEAS in this book have evolved over a number of years, there are an enormous number of wonderful people whose contributions to them have extended over many years and might not initially seem directly related to this book. I readily call to mind Roger R. Miller, who first taught me to value my own ideas; Jean B. Sanville, whose generosity and love of ideas has been invaluable to many areas of my career; Gerald Schamess, who is the most wonderful person in the world with whom to have a dialogue over ideas; Thomas K. Kenemore, who first suggested that I needed a separate concept for the culture created jointly by therapist and client; and Suzanne Whiteley, whose account of her childhood years in Bergen-Belsen provided a powerful stimulus for understanding the interaction between person and environment. There are many more—clients, teachers, students, colleagues, and friends—whose names are not here but who have been important, and I hope they are aware of that.

There are, however, some people who made contributions more directly to the ideas in this book as I was formulating them. Central to this are the members of the Person-in-Environment Group of the Human Behavior and the Social Environment sequence in the School of Social Work at Loyola University Chicago, most of whom met for monthly discussions over a period of more than a year. This group included Ann Bergart, Jude Gonzales, Alan J. Levy, Rose Rogers-Harris, Marion Rosenbluth, Susan Scholten, and Maria Vidal. Frances Stott of the Erikson Institute came late to the group, but still made a significant contribution. Of these, Alan Levy deserves special mention for his collaborative work with me and long-term appreciation and support of my work, which included his assistance in the preparation of my application for a leave of absence to write this.

Jeffrey S. Applegate, Jean B. Sanville, and Elizabeth M. Timberlake all reviewed the plan for the book, not just supporting it but also making suggestions about aspects of its development. Other colleagues and friends read parts of the book and then shared their thoughts about it: Jeffrey Applegate, Martha W. Chescheir, RoseMarie Perez-Foster, Gerald Schamess, and Marcia Spira. The enthusiasm that my editor at Columbia University Press, John Michel, has had for this work gave me a confidence that what I was doing was important.

Catherine Mesavage, my graduate assistant at Loyola University Chicago, helped with finding references for me and working on the indexes. Without the leave given me by Loyola, I would never have had the time to complete this project.

Susan A. McDaniels, whose love and willingness to tolerate my pre-occupations are fundamental to my functioning, has, of course, been crucial.

THE ENVIRONMENT

INTRODUCTION

F OR TWENTY YEARS, postmodernism has been having a dramatic effect on psychoanalytic theory (for example, see Benjamin 1988; Flax 1990; Hoffman 1998; Mitchell 1993; Moore 1999; Schafer 1992; Stern 1997; Stolorow and Atwood 1992). This has resulted in the adoption of varying versions of constructivist or social-constructionist ideas. Indeed, some (Modell 1990) have referred to postmodernism's influence as constituting a major paradigm effect. Interestingly, however, most of these authors have confined their discussions to the reality of the psychoanalytic setting, particularly that of the relationship between the analyst and the patient. Since Freud's conception of treatment rested on the analyst's superior view of reality through which the patient's distortions could be corrected by interpretation, understanding the experience of both patient and analyst is an important—indeed, essential—aspect of clinical theory to address.

Narrowing the theoretical discussions of constructivism and "reality" to that of the treatment session, however, continues a lack of attention to the environment that has been characteristic of analytic theory from its outset. Freud's positivist theory of cognition understood perception to record an accurate picture of external reality that was later distorted by affect and the drives (Schimek 1975). Thus there was no need for the therapist to know much about the patient's external world because, once the analytic process had corrected for the distortions, the patient would be able to recover the originally correct perception. Analytic theory did include a concept of "reality-testing," but for Freud this meant whether the person knew if the stimulus in question came from the external or the internal world, which he saw as quite different entities. In 1974, Robbins and Sadow, noting that understanding reality required far more than this, suggested that psychoanalysis needed a concept of "reality-processing," but this has not been adopted in mainstream psychoanalytic theory.

Although many aspects of Freud's theory have been controversial, his work has served as the model from which other theories have departed. As a result, many of Freud's conceptions have been taken for granted in subsequent work. For example, feminists and many others have been extremely critical of the Oedipus complex, but the criticism has centered on either the sexism involved or the image of fathers as being fundamentally competitive and potentially violent toward their sons. The idea that the external world is necessarily experienced as being harsh and requiring a reluctant compliance in order to ensure survival has largely been overlooked, not discussed either to affirm or to challenge it. This book addresses the role of the environment in psychosocial functioning and psychotherapy, not in psychoanalysis, but it does draw heavily on psychoanalytic theory in its formulations. As considered here, the environment, which includes the realities of social structure and nonhuman objects as well as culture and human beings, plays a highly significant— indeed, a foundational—role in the construction of human identity. It is proposed that in the course of development, human beings first construct a picture of their immediate environment and then construct their identity within that environment. This is the reverse of Freud's assumption that the individual first develops intrapsychically and only later is confronted with the demands of an external reality to which he or she must adapt. When taken seriously, this reversed perspective, acknowledging that the environment has a major role in psychic life, has profound implications for understanding human behavior as well as for a theory of psychotherapy.

THE PROBLEM OF THE EXTERNAL WORLD

CLINICAL SOCIAL WORK, as a profession, has always believed in the importance of the environment and has regarded theories of the "person-in-situation" or the "person–environment configuration" as necessary in order to understand human needs and ways of achieving a comprehension of human beings and their experiences. Yet because paradigms of Western thought separated the individual and the environment into two quite different frameworks, it has been extremely difficult to find a viable bridge between these inner and outer aspects. Thus social work theories have espoused either an intrapsychic approach or a more social approach, with the advocates of each both criticizing and competing with those of the other—even though both sides knew quite well that a more unified approach was really needed. Skilled practitioners in social work have found ways of taking both person and environment into account when actually dealing with clients, but doing so has been a matter of "practice wisdom," not readily translated into a theory.

While Freud paid little attention to the nature of the external world, Hartmann (1958) developed the concept of adaptation, taken from Darwin's theory of evolution. This perspective also has been largely taken for granted within much of object relations theory. Yet there remains a problem with Hartmann's perspective and one of which he was aware. Hartmann knew that it was impossible to speak of adaptation unless one could specify "adaptation to what?" Unable to solve this problem satisfactorily for a theory of psychoanalytic practice, Hartmann adopted the concept of the "average expectable environment"—a solution that probably was not very defensible in Hartmann's time, but is most assuredly not in the contemporary world of complexity and diversity. Whatever else it is, the environment today cannot be described as either average or expectable.

At first glance, it may appear that constructivism eliminates the necessity of dealing with the nature of the external world. After all, constructivism's most fundamental postulate is that human beings cannot achieve what is sometimes called a God's-eye view of the world, cannot know ultimate Truth. Since in postmodern theory any perspective on the external world has to be considered to be only one version of a potentially infinite number of possible perspectives, no theory of psychotherapy can claim to enable practitioners to inform patients of the "true and proper way" to deal with their problems in the world beyond the therapy setting. Further, there are theorists who believe that human beings cannot know even whether there actually is an external world, but this approach is not a very useful one for psychotherapy since clients' problems with functioning in the environment are what has brought them to treatment.

As one of the most prominent postmodern theorists, Kenneth Gergen (1994) is highly critical of the cognitive theories that have been dominant in psychology circles in recent years as well as of claims of authority for the analyst as having superior knowledge of reality in psychoanalytic theories. Gergen calls himself a "social constructionist" and grounds his theory in a critique from postmodern literary theory that argues there is no natural relationship between words and the objects they represent in the external world. He then notes that words do not, in fact, capture a "true representation" of the world, although they may capture a perspective on the world that is dominant in a given culture. Gergen argues eloquently that the understanding of the world that human beings utilize is founded in social consensus and wants therapy to be understood as "enabling clients to participate in the continuous process of creating and transforming meaning" (245). Such a stance is certainly in accord with the trend toward interpersonal and/or intersubjective ideas about the relationship between analysts and their patients and with conceptions of psychotherapy as involving "the creation of meaning" (Saari 1991).

Gergen (1994) also tries very hard to avoid a theory of psychotherapy's having any relationship to a concretely discerned environment. Noting that it is impossible for one person to know another's experience fully, Gergen describes psychotherapy as involving "discourse about experience," rather than experience itself (71). Such psychotherapy nevertheless involves verbal discussion, and its theory must have some way of understanding the literal content of the language used. Here Gergen indicates:

> But as the emphasis shifts to the linguistic construction of reality, illnesses and problems lose ontological privilege. They cease to be "there" as constituents of an independent reality and take their place among the array of cultural constructions. Thus one may speak of problems, suffering, and alleviation, but such terms are always considered to index reality only from a particular perspective. There are no problems beyond a culture's way of constituting them as such. (244)

But this does not avoid the problem of the therapist's need for a view of the cultural environment in order to carry on psychotherapeutic discourse. Further, from a philosophical standpoint it is certainly true that a client's understanding of her problems and suffering can readily be seen as representing only one particular perspective, but for that client, the problems and suffering are very real and must be considered so in any theory of psychotherapy. The need for a serious and empathic approach to the patient's problems is one of the relatively few postulates shared by all theories of psychotherapy. Thus Gergen's theory does not really avoid the need for an understanding of the environment, but only requires that the therapist be aware that the meaning involved is anchored in cultural, rather than in presumed absolute, truth.

Gergen's (1994) social-constructionist perspective, however, presents another problem for theories of psychotherapy: that of the nature of representation. Gergen relies on linguistic theory (Sausseur 1983) in his understanding of language as a system of symbols or codes that refer only to one another and do not have a priviledged relationship with objects in the world. Thus words cannot accurately reflect either the external or the internal world. This is a very important claim because the ability to utilize symbols, primarily in the form of words, although not exclusively in that form, has been a centerpiece of psychoanalytic theory from its inception. Freud believed that it was the ability to link words with thought or ideas that made the difference between that which was conscious and that which was not conscious (Freud 1915/1957; Loewald 1980c). There has been a revolution in linguistic theory since Freud's day, and there is no reason to retain Freud's understanding of the role of language in psychotherapy, but *some* theory of the role of language and the symbols it provides is essential.

How is it that the individual becomes able to capture or express personal experience or meaning in a system of linguistic signs, the reference of which is based on social consensus and which derive their meaning from their relationship to other words in the lexicon? Were this not possible, surely psychotherapy would have been abandoned as worthless shortly after Freud first conceived of it. Yet there is also considerable evidence, particularly from clinical experience, that a patient can use a word, such as *guilt,* that is accurate in terms of its lexical definition and grammatical placement without experiencing the internal state to which it is expected to refer—the consistent use of words in this manner has been called alexithymia, which literally means "words without feelings" (Krystal 1988; Nemiah and Sifneos 1970; Saari 1991).

Nelson's (1985) important work, on which much of the theory in this book has been based, has made it possible to reconcile both Gergen's (1994) contention that words refer only to other words and the clinical understanding of the importance of a client's being able to link inner experiences with words. A developmental psychologist, Nelson has formulated a tripartite theory of meaning that consists of (1) the cognitive representation of meaning for the individual, (2) the communicative context through which the meaning of a word in a specific occasion of use is determined for the individual and that person's interactive partners, and (3) the conventional meaning of a word in the lexicon and in the cultural community at large. Children first learn the use of a word from others in their immediate environment, then come to establish a cognitive referent for the word, and finally learn the interrelationships that the word has within the system of linguistic symbols used in their culture. I have hypothesized elsewhere (Saari 1991) that psychopathology can be seen to involve these three aspects of meaning differentially. Nelson would agree with Gergen that the acquisition of this tripartite meaning system depends on social interactions. Yet Nelson's theory does make the assumption of an existing external world.

Current psychoanalytic theories are similarly unable to avoid the need for a conception of environment. For example, Hoffman (1998), who is probably the most scholarly constructivist among analytic theorists, indicates in a footnote that he disagrees with Gergen's and other theorists' view that reality is "only a function of social consensus"(xxiii). Hoffman does not, however, proceed to discuss how he does view reality. Moore (1999), however, points out that psychoanalysis can hardly expect to help patients with their everyday problems while maintaining a solipsistic view of reality and is quite explicit about the need for an understanding of the nature of the environment within psychoanalytic theory:

> The shift in focus referred to is the by now familiar one away from the evaluation of subjective experience by an objective reality and toward the acceptance of subjective experience as the sole experience of reality to which psychoanalysis has access. Once this shift is accepted, it remains necessary to select from a variety of ways to regard the existence of an external world. Without this selection, no shared theoretical frame of reference for a constructivist psychoanalysis is possible. Construction must be of something, else there is no contextual framework for subjectivity. (139)

Moore, however, then basically sidesteps the problem of that external world by defining the world external to subjectivity as "potential experience" (140). Some years ago, Von Bertalanffy (1968) said that in order to be useful in adaptive behavior human conceptions of the world need not be exact: "It is sufficient that a certain degree of isomorphism exists between the experienced world and the 'real' world, so that the experience can guide the organism in such way as to preserve its existence"

(241). Nevertheless, more attention needs to be paid to conceptualizations of person–environment interactions and their effects than has been done so far. Three major psychoanalytic writers have paid more attention to the role of the external environment than has usually been the case: Harold F. Searles, Donald W. Winnicott, and Hans W. Loewald.

SEARLES'S NONHUMAN ENVIRONMENT

HAROLD F. SEARLES (1960), who was known primarily for his highly skilled work with psychotic patients, devoted an entire book to the environment before the time of postmodernism's influence on analytic theory:

> The thesis of this volume is that the nonhuman environment, far from being of little or no account to human personality development, constitutes one of the most basically important ingredients of human psychological existence. It is my conviction that there is within the human individual a sense, whether at a conscious or unconscious level, of *relatedness to his nonhuman environment,* [and] that this relatedness is one of the transcendentally important facts of human living [italics in original]. (6)

Searles (1960) documented numerous instances in which the environment plays an important role in human life, including concern for pets and the use of similes and metaphors referring to the environment in Romantic poetry. He also said that Harry Stack Sullivan had considered the human being as a part of the world of culture, but that he was saying that humans are "an indissoluble part of the fabric of all created matter" (23). Searles indicated that the nonhuman world makes significant contributions to healthy development through (1) a sense of stability and continuity of experience; (2) the provision of a practice-ground in which the child can develop useful capacities for later interactions in interpersonal relationships; (3) a place in which to find "peace, stability, and companionship at times when his interpersonal relationships are filled with anxiety and loneliness"; (4) the ability to see, in relation to the nonanimate environment, that he is "in various ways powerful, but not omnipotent"; and (5) the ability to create a mature sense of being distinctively human as a part of the natural world (78–99).

In relation to severe pathology, Searles (1960) said:

> I have repeatedly gotten the impression in clinical work that to the seriously ill patient the threat of impending psychosis, for example, conveys terror not merely in that it will bring with it bizarre and frightening and confusing experiences (hallucinations, delusional distortions in his perception of himself and other persons, and so on), but that it will mean the *loss* of familiar relationships with other persons (family members at home, co-workers, and so on) *and of the familiar nonhuman environment* [italics in original]. (19–20)

WINNICOTT'S CONCEPT OF TRANSITIONAL PHENOMENA

THE SECOND WRITER who paid unusual attention to the environment is Donald W. Winnicott, who indicated in the introduction to *Playing and Reality* (1971a) that "cultural experience has not found its true place in the theory used by analysts in their work and in their thinking" (xi). Winnicott proposed that there are three areas of experiencing: an objective view of the external world, a subjective inner world, and a third area that is located between these first two:

> It is usual to refer to "reality-testing," and to make a clear distinction between apperception and perception. I am here staking a claim for an intermediate state between the baby's inability and his growing ability to recognize and accept reality. I am therefore studying the substance of *illusion*, that which is allowed to the infant, and which in adult life is inherent in art and religion, and yet becomes the hallmark of madness when an adult puts too powerful a claim on the credulity of others, forcing them to acknowledge a sharing of illusion that is not their own [italics in original]. (3)

Winnicott's work as both a pediatrician and a psychoanalyst in a hospital in the impoverished East End of London surely brought him into close contact with harsh realities. He refers to "overcrowding, starvation, infestation, the constant threat from physical disease and disaster and from the laws promulgated by a benevolent society" as "the common persecutions" (1971a:142).

Winnicott, however, did not just see the environment as harsh, although he knew that even the best of mothers inevitably falls short of meeting all her infant's needs. When the mother fails, the infant must seek soothing elsewhere and ordinarily encounters useful inanimate objects in the environment, such as a blanket or soft toy, that are more subject to the child's wishes since they have no desires of their own. The infant then can use her own creativity to imbue the object with the soothing qualities of the mother. Henceforth this "transitional object" can be used for consolation whenever the mother is not available. Winnicott's major focus is on the ability of the infant to use environmental objects for play and for creativity. Reality for Freud had a somewhat static as well as a rational character, and the goal of treatment was to liberate human beings from illusion, but, as Greenberg and Mitchell (1983:201) have indicated, Winnicott emphasized almost the precise opposite—a freedom to create illusion.

Winnicott also located culture within the realm of the third area of experiencing, but at times seems to mean the "high culture" of art and religion rather than the everyday culture that directs the mundane activities of life. At other times, he talks of the third area of experiencing as entirely individual. Referring to objective external reality and psychic reality, he said: "By contrast with these, I suggest that the area available for manoeuvre, in terms of the third way of living (where there is cultural experience or creative playing) is extremely variable between individuals. This is because the third area is a product of the *experiences of the individual person* (baby, child, adolescent, adult) in the environment that obtains [italics in original]" (1971a:107). At still other times, culture for Winnicott seems to involve something more like the human meaning system stressed in postmodern theories:

> I have used the term *cultural experience* as an extension of the idea of transitional phenomena and of play without being certain that I can define the word *culture*. The accent indeed is on experience. In using the word culture I am thinking of the inherited tradition. I am thinking of something that is in the common pool of humanity, into which individuals and groups of people may contribute, and from which we all may draw *if we have somewhere to put what we find* [italics in original]. (99)

The place to which Winnicott referred in the italicized section of the quotation is what he called "potential space" between the infant and the mother, a space that exists if the mother is able to respond to the baby's needs and the two can be "alone together." Winnicott's third world of experiencing clearly has roots in social interaction.

For Winnicott, the environment could have negative influences through "environmental impingements" or interferences with the infant's quiescent states by demanding that the infant pay attention to the needs of the caretaker. Such impingements, if characteristic of the relationship between the caretaking environment and the infant, were expected to result in developmental impediments and ultimately in the creation of a pathologic false self, which would serve to protect the true self but could prevent the individual from having a connection with a sense of aliveness and creativity in life. If, however, the mother could allow the child the freedom to play and to create illusion while being protected from such impingements, the development of a true self would be nourished. Winnicott called the facilitating environment that the mother could create for her infant the "holding environment," and then extended these ideas to the environment of the treatment setting by seeing that also as ideally a holding environment.

Winnicott noted both objective external reality and inner psychic reality, but his investment was in the third area of experiencing. There remains a vagueness to the way in which this third area is described—perhaps even almost a mystical character. The engaging manner in which Winnicott described these ideas enhances this character, conveying to the reader that this vagueness is intended and that the third area of experiencing is not to be measured by objectivist, hard science standards. Here, Winnicott, perhaps unknowingly, presaged contemporary theory in both its constructivist and its intersubjectivist turns.

The realms in which Winnicott's ideas about the environment have been useful are far too extensive to take note of here, although they range from the field of child welfare, in which he was an expert, to that of working with elderly nursing home patients who need to retain treasured objects from their home environments in order to maintain contact with a sense of self. Neil Altman's book *The Analyst in the Inner City* (1995) deserves special note as a fine examination of the influence of the environment on psychodynamic psychotherapy in public mental health clinics. Altman does not directly cite Winnicott as a source in his formulation of what he describes as a "three-person" model for treatment: the client, the therapist, and the culture. Yet Winnicott's ideas are so close to some of Altman's that it would be hard to believe that the existent formulation of Winnicott's third area of experiencing did not have at least some influence in Altman's work.

There have, of course, been some criticisms of Winnicott's work. Lorenzor and Orban (1978), for example, indicated that "the inner and outer do not *make up* this intermediate area; instead they *differentiate themselves out of it* [italics in original]" (475).

It is for a closer look at a conception of this possibility that we now turn to Loewald's work.

LOEWALD'S VIEW OF EGO AND REALITY

HANS W. LOEWALD's work was influenced by the ideas of the philosopher Martin Heidegger, who posited, among other things, that the truth of a text is in the interaction between that text and its reader— a precursor to the concept of intersubjectivity (the meaning created in the interaction between two people). Heidegger also saw mind and world as fundamentally inseparable. Loewald's work is, therefore, closer to postmodernism than is the work of other psychoanalysts of his time. In one of his earliest papers, Loewald (1980a) criticized Freud's view of reality as a harsh external world to which the individual must adapt. He noted that Freud's view of reality implies a "fundamental antagonism" (3) between human beings and reality, something he did not believe to be the case:

> Ego, id and external reality become distinguishable in their most primitive, germinal stages. This state of affairs can be expressed either by saying that "the ego detaches itself from the external world," or, more correctly: the ego detaches from itself an outer world. Originally the ego contains everything. Our adult ego feeling, Freud says, is only a shrunken vestige of an all-embracing feeling of intimate connection, or, we might say, unity with the environment. (5)

In other words, the psychological constitution of ego and outer world go hand in hand.

In "Ego and Reality" (1980a), Loewald was addressing primarily the experience of schizophrenic individuals. He pointed out that, because the ego and reality develop together out of a state of primary narcissism, a loss of reality is always also a loss of ego. For this reason, Loewald asserted, the ego need not defend itself from reality, but from the loss of reality. Actually, human beings *do* at times need to defend themselves from reality, as Freud (1920) recognized in his formulations regarding signal anxiety. Yet, as Loewald pointed out, the threat of the loss of a sense of reality is more fundamental, far more disturbing to human functioning than any threat that is experienced as existing in that reality. Searles's (1960) clinical work, documented in *The Non-Human Environment,* illustrated patients suffering from severe mental illness who either had little ability to comprehend the features of their environment or experienced themselves as little different from the nonhuman aspects of their environment. Human beings need an understanding of their surroundings and an explanation for why events in that reality occur. Indeed, if there is no apparent cause or organization in the environment, humans will make one up and use it even if they know that aspects of this understanding are not quite correct. We cannot survive psychologically without such an understanding.

Loewald (1980c) also believed that there are different levels of organization and differentiation of ego/reality functioning that occur as successive stages during the course of a child's development. Severe regression, as occurs in a psychotic breakdown, is the result of a regression of the organization of ego and reality in which the boundary between the two became fused. Interestingly, however, Loewald saw psychic health not as residing at a pinnacle of differentiation from reality, but as resulting from an ability to draw on, flexibly and harmoniously, all the different levels of ego/reality organization in accordance with the nature of the task at hand. Like Winnicott, Loewald understood psychological health to be something more than Freud's rationality.

Reality for Loewald (1980c) also was not the static concept of an average expectable environment, but was conceived of as dynamic:

> The psychoanalytic investigation and understanding of ego development and ego structure, as it progresses, will also lay the foundations for an understanding of the *dynamic* nature of reality. The clearer the distinction between integration as such and defensive types of integration becomes, the more apparent also will be the difference between the idea of an alien, hostile reality (a finished product imposed on the unsuspecting infant from there on and forever after) and the integrated, dynamic reality (forever unfinished)

on the elaboration and organization of which we spend our lives. (32)

The integration of ego and reality for Loewald, therefore, becomes a far more complex relationship than is seen in other psychoanalytic theories.

THE PLAN OF THE BOOK

FOLLOWING THIS INTRODUCTION, the text is separated into three parts, each containing three chapters. Eight of the nine chapters include case illustrations.

Part 1 discusses psychoanalytic and developmental theory, showing that such theory ordinarily has assumed the existence of an environment, but the role of the environment has been taken for granted and therefore unexamined. Concepts of affect, cognition, language and meaning, and culture and identity—as these are understood from a postmodern perspective—are discussed, with a focus on the place of the environment in each. Theories of attachment, social referencing, event representation, and linguistic theories are used in these discussions. Part 1 comes to the conclusion that the environment is so significant to human functioning that a person must first construct an understanding of the immediately surrounding environment before he or she can construct a personal identity.

Part 1 ends with the introduction of Michel Foucault's theory of social control, which becomes the theoretical framework for part 2. Foucault saw psychoanalysis as a mechanism through which the dominant power system could perpetuate itself through the creation of subjectivities. Here, however, I argue that psychotherapy can either dominate or liberate the client, and the three chapters of part 2 focus on ways in which this can occur. Apart from issues of social control, this discussion must be central to current theories of psychotherapy because, once interpretation to a known truth has been disavowed theoretically, some understanding of how to judge what content is therapeutic and what is potentially damaging becomes essential.

Building on the conclusions reached in part 2, part 3 focuses more directly on the implications of an inclusion of environmental considerations for the practice of psychotherapy. These chapters focus on the concordance, or therapeutic culture, created jointly by the client and the therapist, on the importance of the relationship for treatment, and on the place of language and symbolization for treatment.

Finally, in a conclusion, I give additional consideration to a theory of psychotherapy that takes the environment seriously—in particular, a unified theory for all modalities of treatment (individual, couple, family, and group)—and to a theory of the effects of social repression.

PART 1 / THEORY

ONE / THE ENVIRONMENT
IN EMOTIONAL EXPERIENCE

I N CLASSICAL PSYCHOANALYTIC THEORY, it was customary to think of the affective experience of the young infant as being a biologically based element of intrapsychic life. Certainly, the affective experience of the neonate does rely on innate biological systems, but these biological systems simply do not operate in the absence of interactions with an environment. For example, hunger and a state of anger at its persistence, while not reactions to a specific external stimulus, are related to the environment's failure to provide relief for the hunger. Postmodern theory's conception of the importance of context is now pointing out that it is simply not possible to conceive of any human affective reaction that would occur outside an environment. For many years, theories regarding individual development argued for the hegemony either of a drive theory in which inner states determined affective life or of a stimulus–response theory that emphasized the significance of the environment in shaping the behavior and experience of the individual. Current theory, however, is emphasizing a process of continuous interaction between the organism and its environment both in development and in functioning in adult life. For example, Stern (1985) describes the neonate as innately programmed to seek out stimulation from the external world.

Neonates are now known to be quite competent in communicating affectively and in interpreting the affective signals given by their caretakers. The competent mother–baby pair soon develop an entire nonverbal vocabulary with which to understand each other. Infants are, therefore, "thoroughly social" from the very beginning of their lives (Stern 1985: 118). In the foreword to Schore's (1994) extensive exploration of the relationship between affect and brain structure, Grotstein commented, "Furthermore, Freud's concept of drive theory, one of discharge, has become superseded by an object-relations concept; thus, the drives, like the affects, and even like nerves, can now be seen to *communicate* by signals, and later, signs and symbols. The brain, like the mind, is first and foremost an information-seeking and -functioning organ, not primarily a tension-reducing one" (xxiv). Burman (1994) goes further than Grotstein:

> Discussions about the indeterminacy of early responses, then, highlight that there is no such thing as "raw potential": the behaviour we see exhibited by an infant can occur only within a social situation that, firstly, elicits it and, secondly, interprets it, thereby constructing it. It is now well established that environmental events can modify infant behaviour from the earliest moments of life. . . . *One theoretical consequence of this is that there is no easy separation between internal and external,* and that the exhibition of infant behaviour must be regarded as both reactive and interactive [italics added]. (32–33)

The social environment, then, has moved to a position of importance in both child development and adult psychology, with the social environment seen as fundamentally so interactive even with the baby that it is difficult to separate internal and external in causal propositions.

The difficulty in separating internal from external becomes even more apparent in considering Stern's (1985:158) vitality affects. He calls the affects signaled by facial expressions the categorical affects and then adds vitality affects, which have to do with qualities such as timing, tone, intensity, and shape. The vitality affects are omnipresent, but almost always unconscious. We do not, for example, particularly notice that a person moves her arm with rapid acceleration and fullness of display, but will experience it nevertheless as forceful. Indeed, the patterns of affective communication that are laid down in early childhood remain throughout life, but at an unconscious level, and do so not because they are repressed or full of conflict but simply because they are recorded as part of an "implicit memory system" that is functional from birth and is different from the "explicit memory system" to which human beings have conscious access (Amini 1996).

The existence of an implicit memory system is consistent with research into the nature of the human brain that has now concluded that neural structure, perhaps particularly of the right brain where affective functioning is located, is immature at birth and is experience-dependent for its further development. In this regard, Schore (1994) comments that the physical and social context of the developing infant is an essential substratum of the assembling system. The implicit memory constructed in childhood presumably accounts for individual differences in perceptions and in object choices throughout life. Actions and interactions that do not fit well with existent patterning may simply not be noticed, while events that do fit well with the patterning will readily be perceived. Both Nathanson (1992) and Stern (1985) indicate that affective experiences that are not attuned to or amplified by caretaking others do not become conscious. In this manner, then, throughout life the individual will react selectively to environmental events in ways based at least partly on interpretations that had prominence in interactions in early childhood.

The interactive nature of the human infant is also emphasized in current theory because infants are seen as having an "emergent self" (Stern 1985) right from birth; in other words, there is no early symbiotic relationship from which the child must disengage. Experiences of psychological merger are now being interpreted as evidence of an achieved state of relatedness, rather than as a global or an amorphous state from which the child must learn to distinguish self and nonself. After research on newborns that was both extensive and intensive, Demos (1982) concluded that "the human infant is capable of making, and [is] probably perceptually biased to make, distinctions between self and environment, including other humans, right from the beginning" (558). Rather than having a Freudian stimulus barrier, the infant of current theory seeks sensory stimulation and appears to evaluate and hypothesize about the nature of stimuli from birth (Stern 1985). Neonates are curious about and attentive to their environment, both social and nonsocial.

Mutual affect signaling resonates with both infant and caregiver, ordinarily giving pleasure to both parties and amplifying the intensity of the experience. The infant is, however, not fully capable of dealing with this intensity and at times experiences sensory and affective overload, a very distressing state. Affect regulation is, therefore, an area in which it is crucial for infants and young children to receive adult assistance. The mother who holds her upset child closely and sings softly is literally changing the baby's psychological state, acting as a soothing agent or, to use Stern's (1985) term, as a "self-regulating other." The caregiver's regulation of affective states, allowing the child a slowly increasing level of arousal but stepping in to reassure the infant before the intensity becomes unbearable, is essential to the child's ultimate ability to calm herself in the future. Only slowly will the child be able to take over these functions for herself, and the manner in which the child does this will reflect the flavor of the caretaker's interventions.

Current theory, then, puts the influence of the social environment in the life of the young child on center stage. Yet often this social environment is understood basically to mean mother. Siblings, fathers, grandparents, and others, while not as totally neglected in theory as they were twenty-five or more years ago, are still rarely included in studies or discussions about child development, and the physical environment is almost never considered. While from a research perspective the need to limit the field within which variables will be selected is understandable, limiting studies to mother–infant interactions results too often in an overestimation of the mother's influence within the child's milieu, and with it comes the potential for blaming her for any failures or defects. Bronfenbrenner (1979) postulated that the competence of the mother–infant dyad is to a large extent a function of the other dyadic relationships that each of these partners has. Thus the mother's ability to regulate her infant's affect will be highly influenced by whether or not her environment can help to meet her needs, including her own affect regulation. Burman (1994) notes that not infrequently what is understood to be maternal deprivation is really a function of poverty. Thus while theory is now taking into account the immediate interpersonal environment of the infant, any child's environment and its influential qualities remain, in fact, far more complex than has been fully recognized.

ATTACHMENT THEORY

BOWLBY'S (1969) ATTACHMENT THEORY had its roots in observations about what would now be called a pervasive "failure to thrive" in institutionalized infants whose environment lacked stimulation and continuity of caregivers. These children had little investment in their environment, human or nonhuman, and their physical and emotional development was severely delayed or skewed. Bowlby, as well as others who studied these children (e.g., Spitz 1965), focused primarily on the deprivation of human interaction that these children suffered. Bowlby thought that human beings need a close affectional bond with a caretaker in order to develop optimally. Operating within the context of

Darwin's theory of evolution, Bowlby included in his considerations the behavior of nonhuman animals, examining attachments in other species as well as humans. He adopted the term *internal working model* to refer to the aggregated experiences the child has with the caregiver—experiences that are then used by the child as an expectation of what attachment relationships are like.

Following Bowlby (1969), Ainsworth (Ainsworth, Blehar, Waters, and Wall 1978) developed what is now a well-known test for attachment pattern that involves observing the infant's behavior in a laboratory when the mother departs, leaving the child with a stranger, and later returns. From the results of this test, Ainsworth postulated three categories of attachment in the young child: secure, anxious-avoidant, and anxious-resistant. Since that time, Main (Main and Morgan 1996) has identified a fourth group: disorganized-disoriented children. During the 1970s and 1980s, Bowlby's attachment theory was largely ignored by mainstream psychoanalysis as too biological, but during the 1990s it attracted much more attention because of neurological studies indicating that the brain of the neonate actually develops in conjunction with environmental interactions (Amini 1996). Currently, attachment theory is getting even more attention due to studies that indicate the possible transmission of attachment styles from one generation to another. Mothers, for example, when examined on the basis of an interview regarding their own experiences with childhood caretakers, have been found to have attachment styles similar to those of their infants (Fish 1996).

Fonagy (1999) reports that three major longitudinal studies have shown a 68 to 75 percent correspondence between the attachment classification of an individual in infancy and later in adulthood. In explaining how secure attachment may be transmitted from caregiver to child, Fonagy suggests that the caregiver who has a more developed understanding of behavior as influenced by an inner state of mind is more likely to consider behavior in the infant as determined "mentalistically" in the child, thus stimulating the development of a "theory of mind" in the infant. Fonagy notes that children may have an understanding of an independent mind in the other as early as eighteen months.

Attachment theory now has been examined in an impressive number of studies with consistent results. Thus the existence of attachment needs in the neonate can be postulated with a considerable degree of confidence. Nevertheless, the manner in which results have been interpreted has been criticized, primarily on the basis that the strange-situation test, on which so much of this theory rests, may not take into account all the environmental factors that influence the child. Both Burman (1994) and Benjamin (1988), for example, note that a child who is accustomed to a baby-sitter on a regular basis due to the mother's working does not protest the mother's departure as much as does a child not habituated to such events. In this way, children of working mothers may be classified as anxious-avoidant when in fact they may be secure. Such interpretations may, these authors suggest, be used to further conservative political positions that emphasize women's role as homemakers.

INTERSUBJECTIVITY

IN DISCUSSING THE mentalizing of the child, Fonagy (1999) states:

The child's development and perception of mental states in himself and others thus depends on his observation of the mental world of his caregiver. He is able to perceive mental states when the caregiver is in a shared pretend mode of playing with the child (hence the association between pretend and early mentalization), and many ordinary interactions (such as physical care and comforting, conversations with peers) will also involve such shared mentation. This is what makes mental state concepts, such as thinking, inherently intersubjective: shared experience is part of the very logic of mental state concepts. (11)

Intersubjectivity is a concept used in explaining mental processes that is now in vogue with both child developmentalists and psychoanalytic theorists, and as such it is used by different theorists in differing ways. Applegate (1999) notes that Winnicott's work (1958–1986) anticipated much of current thinking about intersubjectivity, and it is those theorists who have built on Winnicott's ideas, specifically Stern (1985) and Benjamin (1988, 1998), who are most useful in considering the importance of the environment in psychological development. This is not surprising since Winnicott's (1975b) well-known concept of transitional phenomena—that is, the child's using an external, soft, nonhuman object to act as a soother in the absence of the mother—involves not a dyadic human interaction but a triad with one element being nonanimate.

Stern (1985) describes intersubjectivity as beginning with an awareness on the part of the infant (around seven to nine months) that the other has a separate mind. He views intersubjectivity as constituted of several pre- or nonverbal processes that include interattentionality, interintentionality, and interaffectivity. Intersubjective processes have major significance for the construction of a richly experienced inner life. These processes, however, should be seen to relate not just to interactions between two people, since the sharing involved is about some object, experience, or event in the environment. Intersubjective processes, therefore, are tripartite. Stern (1985:127) adopts Trevarthen and Hubley's (1978) definition of intersubjectivity as "deliberately sought sharing of *experience about events and things* [italics added]." Further, Stern notes that once an infant becomes capable of intersubjectively experienced states, his mother becomes engaged in the socialization of her child.

Winnicott (1971b) thought the infant's rage at the caretaker, whose devotion is inevitably insufficient to supply whatever is desired immediately, would eventually cause the infant to destroy her representation of the caretaker. Yet if this destruction is survived by the caretaker—that is, if the caretaker neither abandons nor retaliates—then the infant has learned that the other is external, out of the infant's control. The paradox that Winnicott poses here is that it is only through this destruction of the inner object that the infant can come to love, because only an external object can truly be loved. This love is not a love that banishes hate, but a love that can tolerate the hate that is felt for the other and thus can achieve and live with the ambivalence that is characteristic of all mature human relationships. The achievement of ambivalence is pleasurable because with the recognition of the externality of the other comes the joy of being able to share experiences with that other.

Benjamin (1988) builds on this interpretation of Winnicott (1971b) with her concept of recognition, which is the needed experience of seeing and being seen that underlies the ability to share:

In my view, the concept that unifies intersubjective theories of self development is the need for recognition. A person comes to feel that "I am the doer who does, I am the author of my acts," by being with another person who recognizes her acts, her feelings, her intentions, her existence, her independence. Recognition is the essential response, the constant companion of assertion. The subject declares, "I am, I do," and waits for the response, "You are, you have done." Recognition is, thus, reflexive; it includes not only the other's confirming response, but also how we find ourselves in the response. *We recognize ourselves in the other, and we even recognize ourselves in inanimate things* [italics added]. (21)

Note that the recognition that is needed is external—it comes from the environment.

Benjamin (1988) also points out that a theory of intersubjectivity built on Winnicott's ideas and a concept of recognition also requires a different understanding of reality. Reality is now not the "harsh" world to which the Freudian oedipal boy adjusts as he relinquishes his wish to have his mother in view of the castration threat his the father. Reality is now a delightful presence that can be explored, that can potentially be mastered through one's own actions, and that can be shared with an intimate other. The child is now having a "love affair with the world," as Mahler observed and recorded (Mahler, Pine, and Bergman 1975). Mahler, however, was working from a drive-theory perspective and did not pay further attention to the role that the world might play for the infant.

SOCIAL REFERENCING

IN *PLAYING AND REALITY* (1971a), Winnicott asked, "What does the baby see when he or she looks at the mother's face? I am suggesting that, ordinarily, what the baby sees is himself or herself. In other words the mother is looking at the baby and *what she looks like is related to what she sees there* [italics in original]" (112). The infant's picture of self is shaped in large part by what the mother's affective expressions convey, a point also elaborated on as cycles of self and object representations in Jacobson's (1964) theory. The good baby sees mother's proud smile, and the naughty one sees mother's frown of displeasure. Yet studies of social referencing point out that the child sees a good bit more than himself or herself in the mother's affective communications.

Beginning potentially as early as ten months, the child who has acquired the capacity for intersubjective sharing is able to make remarkable use of his mother's face and other means of communicating affect. What is communicated, however, is not just affect, but information about how to behave as well: "In studying very young children, perhaps we have emphasized caregiving at the expense of enculturation. Just as infants (and older children as well) need comfort and care, so too do they need information about environmental events from other people. Not only does the very young child derive emotional and nutritional succor from relationships with adults, but she derives knowledge, social definition, and guidance as well" (Feinman 1992:386).

The experiment involving a "visual cliff," carried out by Emde (1992) and his colleagues, in which a crawling baby was presented with what appeared to be a drop-off (actually clear plastic) between the infant and the mother, is now well known. The baby whose mother smiled and signaled a wish to have the infant come to her would cross the apparent divide, whereas the baby whose mother frowned would not.

Emde (1992:88) has noted that there are different kinds of uncertainties in which social referencing may be used by the child. Initially, there are issues that involve questions of self, such as how his mother feels about him, and safety, as in the cliff experiment. In toddlerhood, there are uncertainties about standards, rules, and prohibitions. Later in the third or fourth year, the child will seek referencing related to issues of roles and relationships. Social referencing has a powerful effect on how human beings come to understand and experience themselves and their environments. Indeed, people can learn to associate pain with pleasure, achievement with humiliation, and many other such apparent paradoxes (Demos 1982).

Demos also has noted that her study of patterns of social referencing in young children makes it clear that a concept of judging the appropriateness of an affective reaction by the nature of the situation itself is quite inadequate. Matching affect with a situation that "should" evoke it fails to take into account the richness of contextual information that will have a bearing on any individual's reaction. The affect evoked will be determined in part by the broader context within which it occurs, the physical state of the person at the time, and the history of that person's involvement in other situations, including those that may be seen as similar by the individual involved even if an external observer would see no similarity.

Social referencing is not confined to childhood. In adolescents, social referencing becomes extremely important in peer-group interactions, sometimes much to the dismay of parents who until that time have been able to ensure that their own principles for behavior have a more central influence. Feinman (1992) reminds us that social referencing also has a direct influence on self-esteem in regard to performance or efficacy. The judgment, or perhaps only the expected judgment, of others on one's ability to perform important skills is a part of daily life. Nathanson (1992) here would point out that the person's experience or expectation of negative judgments by others makes that person vulnerable to painful experiences of shame. Social referencing, then, is a prominent type of communication used throughout the lifespan, existing as an important factor of motivation for thought and behavior.

Feinman (1992) notes that, since it is not just a one-way communication, perhaps social referencing should be called negotiation. The mother uses referencing as well, watching her baby for cues regarding how he or she is feeling or thinking. Is he getting overexcited enough to require her to call a halt to the action? Is she attracted to and about to touch something that might be dangerous? Social referencing can be looked at as a foundation on which the shared meaning we call culture is created and transferred from one person to another, from one generation to another.

THE DEVELOPMENT OF EMOTION

IN TUNE WITH THE scientistic thinking of his time, Freud believed that perception was accurate but was subsequently distorted by the affects and need states of the individual. Thus initially, psychoanalytic treatment was expected to do away with the affective distortions of the percept and restore the original objective perception. In current theory, however, affect is not thought to distort perceptions, which we now believe to have been biased from the beginning. In general, there is acceptance of the idea that affect and cognition are not at all the kind of separate and opposing functions that Freud understood them to be (Stern 1985). Indeed, Bruner (1986) has indicated that we do not perceive, think, or feel separately, but we "perfink"(69); that is, we do all these things simultaneously, and they are separable only in our conception of them. While Freud thought of human beings as necessarily wary about becoming overwhelmed by too much emotion, Seton (1981) has noted that we like to experience feelings, even if they are sometimes painful, because they tell us we are alive.

Affective/cognitive processes are now often thought to have a developmental course during the childhood years. Tomkins (1962) proposed that facial expressions denoting human affects are innate and universal. These facial expressions were interpreted cross-culturally as showing interest–excitement, enjoyment–joy, surprise–startle, fear–terror, distress–anguish, anger–rage, dissmell, disgust, and shame–humiliation (Nathanson 1992). Following Tomkins, others, including Izard (1971), have found that facial expressions for sadness, anger, disgust, contempt, surprise, happiness, and fear are interpreted similarly throughout the world (Amini 1996). However, we do not know what the baby is actually feeling when these expressions are displayed. Mothers nevertheless interpret their newborns' faces as conveying a message about the inner state of the infants, thereby encouraging their communicative use. In turn, then, the communicative use shapes the baby's interpretation of the facial expression as having the affective coloring initially given to it by the mother.

Basch (1976) builds on Tomkins's (1962) work, seeing *affect* as highly biological, not even involving conscious experience. Basch uses the word *feeling* for the experience when the person is aware of it, which begins in the latter part of the oedipal stage. Finally, the word *emotion* is defined: "Emotions are subjectively experienced states and always related to a concept of self vis-à-vis some particular situation" (768). Thus emotions, which develop in late latency or early adolescence, involve cognitive appraisals in relation to an environmental condition. Increasingly, emotions are being viewed in this manner. Kernberg (1990) does not propose a developmental course, but has referred to affects as "complex psychic structures that are indissolubly linked to the individual's cognitive appraisals of his immediate situation"(125). Krause (1998) has said, "Emotions are thus not simply bodily or physiological states into and out of which individuals move. It is more useful to understand emotions as processes of appraisal and communication which draw on cultural themes of meaning and which are reconstituted, experienced and changed in the course of evolving social relationships"(64).

Blatt (1974) constructed a developmental course for affect, relying on Piaget's (1962) cognitive theory, Werner and Kaplan's (1963) theory of symbolization, and Mahler's object-relations theory (for an explanation of Blatt's theory, see also Lane and Schwartz 1987). Blatt's conception of this developmental course involved the idea that the individual's ability to perceive characteristics in other human beings is limited to psychological aspects that are experienced internally. Thus at the most primitive level, the individual can see others only through the lens of how useful or not useful this person is for his or her own needs. The development was then thought to proceed through a stage in which external concrete aspects of the person would be noticed, to one in which actions of the person would be noticed, to one in which internal experiences would be seen but only globally, and finally to one in which the person would be seen as a more complex person who experienced ambivalence and who changed over time. Blatt's theory, however, deals only with perceptions of the human objects in the environment.

Nathanson (1992), who accepts Basch's (1976) ideas regarding the development and types of affect, adds mood. He thinks a mood may last much longer than an affect, even several days or more. Mood, he says, occurs when a current affect becomes connected to a memory of some earlier experience. The memory of the earlier experience may or may not be conscious. Nathanson remarks:

Whereas affect is biology, emotion is biography.

Affect is about unvarying physiological mechanisms. To fit our definition of emotion an affect must be placed within a script or a story. (50)

In summary, then, current conceptions do not split affect, cognition, and perception, which are thought of as integrated into a unified line that has a developmental course and an inherent relationship to the environment. Increasingly, this phenomenon is referred to as "meaning."

TWO / THE DEVELOPMENT OF MEANING

U NTIL TWENTY-FIVE YEARS AGO, developmental psychology thought of the single, external object as the primary base for representation and thus the fundamental building block for cognition. There was an assumption, usually not noted, that the child learned about the characteristics of an object and then was able to build an image of the whole by putting together a number of objects. In psychoanalytic theory, the term *object* usually referred to a person, not an inanimate thing, but the principles of how a child composed a picture of self and the external world were similar to those of developmental psychology. In a recent shift in understanding, representation takes the form of an event, initially taking place in childhood, experienced as a global whole from which objects may later be abstracted. One fairly obvious advantage of event representations for psychoanalytic theory is that actions, previously neglected in psychoanalytic theory except for "acting out," become a significant part of the representations of the world. The concept of event representations, however, also allows for the recognition that events always occur in a context, or culture, an inclusion that is of major import for understanding the psychological significance of the environment.

The shift of focus from object to event has already begun to influence psychoanalytic conceptualization. This can be seen in Stern's (1985) use of episodic memory, by which he means that the experience of any event is registered in the mind as a whole from the outset—that is, not as a series of perceptions that become linked as a whole by later cognitive processing. The child's representation of his mother, therefore, is not an objective picture of her, but is based on that child's experience of his mother. Since the child has many experiences with his mother, the representation created out of experiences with her becomes generalized in a way that may, in fact, not coincide with any single encounter with her, but does capture the major aspects of most such encounters. It is, then, from representations of experiences with the world that the child comes slowly to construct an understanding of the nature of the environment.

The concept of event representation actually began as a part of schema theory in the work of Schank and Abelson (1977), who formulated a concept of a "script"—a temporally ordered sequence of actions that are appropriate to a particular context and are organized around a goal. A script specifies roles, props, and contexts as well as options regarding what things or persons can be used as alternatives in the action. Children's early scripts deal with actions that are common and repeatable within daily life and are not collections of discrete experiences, but generalizations built on similar experiences. Perhaps one way to characterize scripts is to note that they are how the family dog knows what will happen next. There is a series of actions that regularly take place in a particular order so that the animal knows what is to come next without having to know language.

Schank and Abelson (1977) arrived at the concept of scripts from a base of both artificial intelligence and linguistics; essentially, they were asking themselves what an understander needs to know in order to fill in the gaps created by inferences in human communication. Although Schank and Abelson did not concern themselves with psychopathology, the inability to fill in such gaps can often be seen in problems encountered by individuals with schizophrenia. In a cooking class, for example, Matthew had been told to cook some frozen peas following the instructions on the box. Matthew followed the instructions with the utmost care, but because they did not say that the peas should be taken out of the box, he put the box itself into the boiling water. Of their script theory, Shank and Abelson said:

> By subscribing to a script-based theory of understanding, we are making some strong claims about the nature of the understanding process. In order to understand the actions that are going on in a given situation, a person must have been in that situation before. That is, understanding is knowledge-based. The actions of others make sense only insofar as they are part of a stored pattern of actions that have been previously experienced. Deviations from the standard pattern are handled with some difficulty. (67)

Schank and Abelson's claims have indeed been revolutionary in the understanding of human behavior, and it is likely that the explanatory power of a script-like theory of representation is not yet fully appreciated.

Schank and Abelson (1977) were aware that scripts are important in understanding stories, specifically because they allow the storyteller to leave out unimportant, essentially boring, information and stick to the significant aspects of the event. Mandler (1984) took the relationship between scripts and stories further, noting that scripts form the basis for story structure. Mandler also discussed the idea of "scenes" (i.e., the spacial context within which something may occur) and noted that, once having a schema for a scene—a living room, perhaps—one can know whether or not a particular object would belong there: a chair would belong, but a motorcycle ordinarily would be considered unusual.

Nelson (1986) and her colleagues have noted that children learn through *social participation*. As early as age three, a child can provide a generalized report of what happens at a birthday party even if the child has experienced only one such event. If the event requires sequencing, as does eating at a restaurant, the child may forget some aspect of what occurs—ordering the food, perhaps. However, children never get the sequence wrong: one cannot eat the food before ordering it. Because children's event representations are constructed through social participation, the information in the representation is invariably culturally determined. Some children may include a piñata at the birthday party in their event representations, but others would not.

Stories are built on event representations (Seidman, Nelson, and Gruendel 1986). Before age eight at the earliest, children asked to produce a story will give what is really an event representation: "Johnny went to the store. He was going to buy some bread. He bought candy instead. That's all." The "That's all" comes because there is no end point to the story, and therefore the listener cannot automatically tell when the events conclude. In contrast to an event representation, a story has an evaluative end point and therefore does not need the "That's all." "Johnny was supposed to buy some bread, but when he got to the store he wanted some candy so he bought that instead" is a simple story. It includes an implied evaluation or end point: perhaps Johnny has been bad (he did something he was not supposed to do), and Johnny is now a person with an inner life (he wanted candy and allowed this desire to take precedence over what he was supposed to do). Since narrative form is now believed to be natural to human constructions of identity (Bruner

1990; Polkinghorne 1988; Schafer 1992), the role of event representations as the foundation for stories is of no small importance.

Nelson and her colleagues have carried out an impressive amount of research on event representations (e.g., Hudson, Shapiro, and Sosa 1995; Hudson and Sheffield 1998; Kuebli and Fivush 1994; Lucariello, Kyratzis, and Nelson 1985; Seidman, Nelson, and Gruendel 1986; Yu and Nelson 1993). Nelson (1986) has noted: "A summary of the functions of scripts for the individual, then, includes predicting action and interaction, supporting the interpretation of discourse, action and task demands, organizing memory, making plans, and serving as a base for the derivation of abstract knowledge structures" (17). The introduction to this volume noted that in Nelson's (1985) tripartite theory of meaning, the infant first achieves shared reference, which serves as the context for meaning with communicative partners. This is very important for a theory of psychotherapy because it provides a direct linkage between the extent and nature of human relationships and the acquisition of meaning.

Additionally, in psychotherapy event representations underlie the little vignettes of memory or experience that are so meaningful in relation to a client's current difficulties.

An attractive young man in his early thirties, Andres entered treatment for depression following the breakup of his marriage, which had lasted less than a year. Andres had come from a privileged background and had been given what amounted to a considerable fortune by his family. Well educated in high-status universities and clearly intelligent, Andres nevertheless had not been very successful in his business career. Over the course of treatment, knowledge of his difficulties at work appeared to indicate that he had trouble knowing how to deal with people.

Before his marriage, Andres for many years had dated Kelly, a young woman from his hometown. His family had expected him to marry her, but he had not wanted to do so. Kelly also came from wealth, and Andres—who indicated that he carried a lot of guilt about having so much money and wanted to use his life to do something to help others less fortunate—saw that early marriage prospect as meaning he would live like his very proper upper-class parents.

Andres had met his wife, Jean, at a restaurant in the business district of the city. Like Andres, Jean worked in the area, but she had come from a lower-class background. Jean had worked hard to attain a college degree and still had considerable debt. Before their marriage, Andres and Jean had had a whirlwind three-month courtship, and at that time they had seen themselves as very much in love. Attempts to get from Andres descriptions of what Jean was like as a person were quite unsuccessful, however. For example, he had little understanding of why she had left him except that she did not like that he cried easily, something he indicated he knew most men did not do but he thought was simply a sign of what a "sensitive" and caring man he was. Andres had no understanding whatever that Jean initially may have found the lifestyle to which he was accustomed intoxicating or that she later may have found the world he and his family lived in stressful.

Two vignettes Andres gave me stand out as significant in my understanding of how serious his psychological difficulties were and of how the patterns of interaction in his family may have contributed to his problems. In the first story, Andres flew home for an anniversary celebration for his parents. He had expected that this would entail only his siblings and two to three couples who were close friends of his parents. Arriving on the afternoon of the party, he discovered that it was to be a very large event, and this angered him because he had no chance to prepare for it. At the celebration, guests were giving toasts to his parents. Andres, unable to think of a toast that he could give, sat at the head table, in front of the guests, for the three to four hours of the party feeling humiliated.

The second vignette came after I had been trying very hard to get Andres to tell me something about what his relationship with his parents was like. Andres was the middle child of three; he had an older brother, who was gay and who ultimately died of AIDS, and a younger sister. He described his mother and his brother as being close; his father and sister were also close. The story concerned his sister's wedding, which took place in a resort area distant from the family home and in the last year of his brother's life. The brother, not feeling well, excused himself from the reception and took one of the two cars the family had rented to return to the hotel in which the family was staying. With the brother gone, Andres's parents began arguing, the mother saying that they should go back to the hotel to take care of him if needed and the father insisting that they could not leave their daughter's wedding reception. When the mother won the argument and the parents decided to leave, Andres was left not knowing what to do. He did not want to leave the reception, but if his parents took the one remaining car he would have no way of getting back to the hotel. Thus he left with his parents, sitting alone and ignored in the backseat for the extended drive, with his parents in front, each angrily accusing the other of not caring about the child with whom the other parent was unaligned. Andres's experience was that neither parent was aligned with him.

—

In considering those two vignettes, note that—because I have formed my own generalized event representations of differences in the world-view of upper- and lower-class people and of anniversary celebrations and toasts—it was possible for me to know what *might* have occurred and to know what Andres's psychological difficulties *might* have been. I could wonder why it was so very hard for Andres to come up with a simple toast to his parents in the course of three or four hours; I might have thought that perhaps he had difficulty in utilizing cognitive operations on his event representations. And if Andres's story of his parents arguing while he sat alone in the backseat was indeed typical of his relationship with them, by using my own cognitive abilities I could construct a picture of what might have occurred in Andres's development.

THE SIGNIFICANCE OF HUMAN RELATIONSHIPS

ALTHOUGH I HAD no information about what Andres's relationship with his parents was like other than the little he was able to tell me and what I experienced in his manner of relating to me, I am assuming that his experienced difficulties in the creation of meaning imply the possibility that something went wrong in this area in his early development. This assumption is based on the idea that, in accord with Nelson's (1985) theory, a child first develops the ability to share reference with communicative partners. Human beings are social creatures, something that current psychoanalytic theory is increasingly recognizing as fundamental to intersubjectivity.

Werner and Kaplan (1963) agreed with Piaget (1962) that action is an important factor in early cognitive development and noted that, at first, the neonate's world is full of "things-of-action"—things that can be encountered and influenced through movements. However, Werner and

Kaplan thought that, at about eight months, the infant's world changes to "objects-of-contemplation"—things that can be examined and shared with a significant other. Aware of Winnicott's (1975b) concept of transitional objects, Werner and Kaplan saw a similarity between it and their idea of objects-of-contemplation. The healthy child is a social being who experiences joy in interactions with human others and comes to find pleasure in sharing an experience of the environment with his or her caretakers.

From the contemplative situation, as was discussed in relation to social referencing, the child learns what to notice in the world and how to feel about it. However, the child also learns how to interact with others in relation to the external world, something that has perhaps been less commonly noted in developmental and clinical literature. Yet these patterns of interpersonal interaction, while certainly not immune to later alteration, can persist throughout life and thus have a major influence on how extensively aspects of the environment will be noticed and shared with others. The affective quality with which such explorations will be colored can, of course, also be influenced. For example, the child whose caretaker finds pleasure in the youngster's discoveries will likely continue to enjoy new objects and experiences, while the child whose caretaker sees the world as dangerous may continue to see danger in the world, and the child whose mother pays little attention to those early discoveries may later be less likely to share discoveries with others. In regard to the relational aspects of representational processes, Fast (1998)—who uses Nelson's work in her formulations—suggests that for psychoanalysis a focus on relational interactions rather than on sensory impressions is important. She sees this interactive relationship as "a dynamic scheme of personally motivated interaction rather than a pair of [self and other] representations joined by a hyphen" (32).

Nelson (1985) points out that human perception does not result in an accurate copy of the world, but is made unique by factors such as present biological functioning, biological state, a history of exposure to similar events, and the point of view from which the event is perceived. What is felt and recorded in memory is not the "real world," but the individual's experience with the real world. Thus the child whose mother is typically uninterested in the child's discoveries may well not know that his mother's lack of interest stems not from a lack of care for the child, but from exhaustion due to the necessity of working two jobs in order to support the family. Representation, therefore, is not an accurate reflection of the world, but a recording of the individual's experience—something that will be heavily influenced by the context of the human relationships in the early world of the child.

While the development of cognition makes possible the manipulation of representations, including the separating out of particular aspects of experience for examination in relation to information acquired following the particular event, cognitive operations can still take into consideration only that which was actually perceived. For example, the child whose mother was constantly exhausted may feel more positively about his mother once he has come to understand the enormous pressures that economic circumstances have forced on her, but may still have difficulty recalling an image of his mother as caring.

THE CONSTRUCTION OF THE WORLD AND THE SELF

IN A FASCINATING single-case study, Nelson (1989) and her colleagues examined the bedtime monologues of a toddler named Emily between the ages of twenty-one and thirty-six months. Emily's parents, who were academics, agreed to place a tape recorder under the child's crib to record her talk around bedtime, both in dialogue with the parent who put her to bed and in monologue before sleeping. Interestingly, Emily used more highly developed speech patterns in her monologues to herself than she did in the dialogues with her parents. The parents tended to focus frequently on events that were expected to occur after Emily woke up. Although at times Emily referred in her monologues to the content of the dialogues with her parents, for the most part she talked not about the future, but about what had already happened in her life. She appeared to be trying to master her understanding of how the world around her worked. In other words, Emily seemed to be constructing event representations. She was developing and using the cognitive skills to create her own meaning, the second element in Nelson's tripartite theory of meaning,

During the time of the tape-recording, Emily experienced the birth of a brother. The event had a major effect on her life, especially since she was moved to another bedroom, farther from her parents' room, in anticipation of the baby's arrival. From Freudian theory, one would expect to hear a lot about sibling rivalry. Yet the brother is hardly mentioned in Emily's monologues, which focus instead on everyday routines. This does not mean that Emily will experience no sibling rivalry, but that at the time of the recording the birth of Emily's brother was not the part of the world she was trying to understand. Nelson (1989) notes three themes that emerge in the content analysis of the monologues: (1) the world of people, things, and activities in which Emily participates; (2) the task of mastering language; and (3) "the discovery of herself as a thinking, feeling, acting person in the world of other people who think, feel, act, and interact with her" (20). Nelson also indicates:

> From this analysis of content it is apparent that the major topics and themes of Emily's talk involve the effort to make sense of her experience, to construct a model of the world that will permit her to anticipate what will happen and thus enable her to take her part in events effectively. Her parents actively assist her in this by their extensive talk about what will happen, while Emily contributes an independent account of what has happened because—together with parental explanations—it serves as a foundation for an understanding of what *will* happen. Norms and scripts are built from what has happened and has been understood previously, and once constructed, they take their place in the general knowledge model and the child no longer seems to need to discuss them. (41)

Burner and Lucariello (1989) refer to Emily's accomplishments in the monologues as a "triumph of ordinariness" (96).

The strong implication of the study of Emily's monologues is that in order to know *who she is,* Emily must first understand the world in which she lives. Only then can she understand her place in that world. This is a highly significant difference from more classical psychoanalytic assumptions that the intrapsychic world is determined by an internal biological inheritance that is "destiny" and that the surrounding "harsh reality" is encountered and dealt with by a reluctant accommodation in the face of oedipal struggles. Knowledge of the world is essential to the very foundation of understanding ourselves. In the context of this developmental perspective, Loewald's (1980a) insight that a loss of reality is always also a loss of self takes on a new depth of meaning.

The original interrelationship of self and environment, based on the child's active participation within the environment and the event representations that are derived from that participation, becomes even more significant when the place of event representations in the construction of categories is understood. From as early as Bleuler's (1924) studies of schizophrenia, it has been recognized that the inability to maintain appropriate categories with consistent defining characteristics is a fundamental symptom of mental illness. Thus in proper categories, inclusion must be based on the same characteristic(s) for each of the items, and an adult who thinks that she can go out and buy "a furniture" will be considered crazy. It has also been recognized that there is some connection between the ability to categorize and the experience of an intact self, but the exact nature of that connection has been elusive.

Piaget (1962) believed that the child's ability to deal with categories does not begin until well into school age, and the presentation in which he housed this theory is long and so complicated as almost to defy comprehension. In schema theory, on the contrary, children can use basic categories from a much earlier age, and the theoretical explanation is remarkably simple. Event representations involve *slots* in which a number of equivalent items can be placed (Nelson 1986). For example, games at a birthday party might include drop-the-handkerchief, pin-the-tail, or any number of similar ones. Food at a restaurant might include hamburgers, hot dogs, or chicken. All the items in a slot that would be correctly understood as adequate substitutes for another item in that slot make up a category. Young children need practice to master which items are culturally appropriate replacements in their event representations, which is at least partially done through the earliest form of humor in young children. Here the child will put something that is highly inappropriate into a slot and think it wildly funny: "Johnny ate a mosquito-burger for dinner last night" or "There was an elephant having dinner at Johnny's house." This sort of humor ordinarily has far less appeal to adults.

For Nelson (1986), then, event representations provide children with a number of natural opportunities to learn simple classifications of everyday items. Categories are therefore operative by age three, with the more abstract, taxonomic classifications being learned later. Note here also that classifications are clearly based on cultural, environmental knowledge, not on an abstract understanding of the categories inherent in the "real world" as understood objectively or scientifically. Lakoff (1987), whose theory of categorization is similar in many respects to Nelson's, says, "Thus the relevant notion of a 'property' is not something objectively in the world independent of any being; it is rather what we will refer to as an *interactional property*—the result of our interactions as part of our physical and cultural environments given our bodies and our cognitive apparatus. . . . As long as we are talking about properties of basic-level objects, interactional properties will seem objective" (51). Categorization at a basic level, according to Lakoff, Nelson, and a number of other developmental psychologists, including Stern (1985), is operative in the child from very early in childhood.

Basic-level categorization as an early capability gains yet more significance when it is understood that "what mothers think" and "what fathers do" are slots in early event representations and thus are created as categories. "What I think, feel, and do" are also slots. So is "How others treat me." Now it becomes possible to assume, knowing of Andres's ride in the car backseat, that he might fundamentally see himself as someone who was of little importance to others. A sense of self or identity is a basic-level category created out of slots in early event representations: it is made up of "what it is like being me" in the various scripts in which the child has a role. The environment and one's place in it is, therefore, a fundamental element in our constructions of ourselves.

Before proceeding to an examination of the third element in Nelson's (1985) theory of meaning, one further point has to be made. The toddler Emily was advantaged in her creation of event representations because her life was relatively predictable, with myriad opportunities to construct and reflect on event representatives that do require some repeatability for their formation. Other children may not be so fortunate and so may have less ability to create pictures of both self and environment. Nelson (1986) remarks: "A child who faces a world that is constantly changing, that does not provide the kind of repeatable event structure that makes a stable event representation possible, cannot achieve this kind of stability. We call this the *chaos factor* and speculate that it may have broad repercussions for the impairment of cognitive functioning when stable representations are not established and thus do not become available for cognitive processing" (246–247). Thus the child whose early life experience is full of chaos may have deficits in the cognitive skills that can lead to "success" in life.

LANGUAGE AS THE THIRD COMPONENT OF MEANING

THE THIRD COMPONENT of meaning in Nelson's (1985) tripartite theory is that of language (sense), which makes possible participation in the meaning system within the wider cultural community with people who, as individuals, are unknown. The particular words the child learns are a part of an entire linguistic system shared by an ethnic or a national group. Commenting on this process, Nelson notes: "Language meaning proceeds from the outside inward through reference to the real world" (96). Language is learned from the caretaker(s). Thus children's first use of language is activity-bound and itself an element of the activity through which the child learns to share experiences with communicative partners. However, as the child constructs event representations, she or he also discovers that the words can be used to communicate with those unknown others who are a part of the world beyond the immediate family circle.

Language has often been seen as a part of Winnicott's (1975b) transitional phenomena. As we have seen, Werner and Kaplan (1963) regarded verbal language as a system of symbols that originate in the contemplation of objects with a significant other. Along these lines, Stern (1985:172) notes that the word originates from the outside, with the mother, but can connect with a thought and therefore is a transitional phenomenon in Winnicott's sense, occupying a space between mother and child. Seeing language as part of an intersubjective space, Benjamin (1998) says:

> Language is the heir to the transitional space inasmuch as we see it less in its Lacanian sense as subjecting the individual to the symbolic structure, and more relationally as forming the medium of the subject's acting on and interacting with the world. Hence it constitutes a space of fluctuating convergence and divergence between inner and outer. When we consider language as speech between subjects, we modify our understanding of the move from body to speech. Speech no longer figures as the activity of a subject empowered to speak, but as a possibility given by the relationship with a recognizing other. Or, we could say, speech is conditioned by the recognition between two subjects, rather than a property of the subject. (28)

In its role as a semantic system utilized to connect with unknown others in the larger community, however, language must become somewhat separated from the more intimately shared context in which meaning began. Thus part of the learning through the creation and refinement of event representations, as they are subjected to individual cognitive processes, involves the ability to distinguish purely personal or local meaning from that which is useful within the culture as a whole. Thus the preschool child begins to utilize language to distinguish between meaning that is personal to herself and that in which others around her share. At the same time, the child slowly masters the capacity to utilize abstractions and categories with words that, like *furniture*, have no real referents in the concrete material surround.

One of the major advantages of the semantic aspects of language is that words can be used to call up objects not present in the immediate context and to manipulate objects and events in ways that are not possible in the "real world." Thus by adolescence, the child ordinarily has learned to use words to envision imaginary worlds that may be soothing and reassuring, but may also be frightening. It was the use of words in this more abstract sense, not referring to concrete external materiality, that led Saussure (1959) to note that words refer only to other words. Gergen (1994) relies on this conception of language to build a strict social constructionism—one that holds there is no relationship between the use of words and the external world, and indeed this is certainly the case when one considers the construction of a "truth" in an objective sense. Gergen's ideas, however, formulated more in philosophical terms than in clinical observations, fail to consider the complexity of human meaning—for example, reference and denotation, the first two levels of Nelson's (1985) theory. Gergen's ideas, therefore, are not adequate as a guide for psychotherapy. Although Gergen wants to see language as rooted in social processes, a theory based solely in a strictly Saussurean conception of language fails to capture either individual experience or the significance of the external world, including even the social processes that are important to Gergen.

Within Nelson's (1985) tripartite theory of meaning, however, word definition is reached through a social process. Furthermore, words help to determine both that which is to be noticed and that which is not significant. For example, Tessler and Nelson (1994) report a study in which ten pairs, each pair consisting of a mother and her three-and-a-half-year-old child, visited a museum, with all the talk between mother and child being recorded. One week later, the children were interviewed—the mothers not being present—about what they remembered having seen in the museum. No child reported having seen anything that had not been talked about. Thus language is an essential tool used by early caretakers (as well as others) for acculturating the child. As Stern (1985) notes, language both reveals and conceals because it teaches the child both what to know and what to ignore. In a similar sense, language can both serve a differentiating and individuating function (through allowing for increasingly detailed discriminations about self and the external world) and connect the child with the surrounding culture.

Recent study of language and meaning has opened up new avenues to the exploration of the relationship between human beings and the environment. Even so, there undoubtedly still are limitations in the scope of knowledge we have been able to achieve. Burman (1994), for example, notes:

> The idea that all language learning is a dyadic process is a very particular cultural construction that reflects the Eurocentric and class biases of child language research. While most children learn to talk in polyadic situations (interacting with more than one adult, and with other children), and this may play a much more active role in the process by which children pair utterances with meaning, child language research routinely screens out all language partners other than the mother and child. (115)

Cultural contexts are therefore important both to the development of the child and to later meaning systems utilized by an adult.

T HE SYMBOLIC INTERACTIONIST Howard Becker (1986) has
defined culture as "the shared understandings that people use to
coordinate their activities" (15). Culture, therefore, can be seen as
the more generalized understandings at which people in a particular
environment arrive through intersubjective processes of sharing. Becker
also regards culture as always a work in progress:

> People create culture continuously. Since no two situations are alike,
> the cultural solutions available to them are only approximate. Even
> in the simplest societies, no two people learn quite the same cultural
> material; the chance encounters of daily life provide sufficient vari-
> ation to ensure that. No set of cultural understandings, then, pro-
> vides a perfectly applicable solution to any problem people have to
> solve in the course of their day, and they therefore must remake
> those solutions, adapt their understandings to the new situation in
> the light of what is different about it. Even the most conscious and
> determined effort to keep things as they are would necessarily
> involve strenuous efforts to remake and reinforce understandings so
> as to keep them intact in the face of what was changing. (19)

In this conception, culture is not only a meaning-making process, but
one that is constantly changing in the face of events of everyday life.
Thus each individual is continually involved both in behaving in accord
with cultural definitions of reality and in altering such definitions when
they do not work well.

Traditionally, an intrapsychically oriented theory for psychotherapy
has viewed culture as something external to the human being—indeed,
even external to the clinical situation—something "out there" that may
have some bearing on the patient's behavior, but is clearly of a different
order of understanding than, and probably intellectually inferior to,

psychoanalytic theory's understanding of the intrapsychic world. Yet, as we have seen, culture, understood as constructed through event representations, is an integral part not only of the patient's conception of the world but also of the person's very self-definition. The external conception of culture in psychoanalytic theory is slowly changing in the face of the diversity now common even in Western societies. Adams (1996), for example, has remarked, "For me, the clinical *is* the cultural. Psychoanalysis does not so much move away from the clinical context in order to encounter cultural phenomena as it encounters cultural phenomena *in* the clinical context [italics in original]" (240).

In Nelson's (1985) tripartite model of meaning, all knowledge is cultural, not just in the sense of event representations that are a part of the immediate social surround, but also in language's embeddedness in the meaning system of the wider surrounding community. Actually, knowledge is cultural in a third way because cognitive operations carried out on the person's event representations will inevitably reflect patterns of interactions with communicative partners. In fact, Bruner (1986:122) has asked whether social concepts are located in the individual's head, in the world, or in interpersonal negotiation and indicated that the answer would have to be in interpersonal negotiation. In accord with Becker (1986), Bruner sees culture in a constant process of re-creation as new circumstances, problems, and technologies appear. And since psychotherapy can readily be understood as a process through which clients examine, create, and refine their identities and their comprehension of the world, it is not much of a leap to understand psychotherapy itself as an interpersonal negotiation of social meaning.

Understanding psychotherapy as having roots in cultural interactions is slowly becoming acknowledged. For example, the psychoanalyst Irene Fast (1998) recently discussed the unconscious as formed through engagements with the external world:

> Unconscious (id) experiences are not endogenous, patterned by bodily drives, but are patterned in individuals' engagements with their worlds. They do not occur in peoples's lives as eruptions from the depths of psychic structure, but are self-world engagements that are split off from the individual's other ways of selving. People's ways of going about things in their everyday activities exist side by side with their other self-world engagements but are subjectively isolated and carry little or no sense of self. (110)

POSTMODERNISM AND CULTURE

POSTMODERNISM IS RAPIDLY becoming the framework within which theories of psychoanalysis and psychodynamic psychotherapy are being framed (for an excellent review of postmodern concepts and their implications for psychoanalytic work, see Shawver 1996). Although the postmodern turn initially created some conflicts for medically trained psychoanalysts who saw themselves as scientists, it has received increasing acceptance due to its advantages for conceptions of clinical work. For example, narrative and hermeneutic ideas are a far better fit for understanding clinical processes than are presumed universal principles of scientific laws (Aron 1996; Fast 1998; Hoffman 1998; Moore 1999; Schafer 1997). Since psychoanalysis involves a two-person interchange, discussions of dialogue are becoming common in the literature (Mitchell and Aron 1999), and the multiplicity of meaning has led to conceptions of multiple selves (Bromberg 1998; Slavin 1996).

Postmodern insistence on the importance of context for interpretation, along with increasing cultural diversity within the United States, is the predominant reason for the current attention to culture within psychoanalytic theory. Understanding the fundamental processes in psychotherapy as involving the creation of meaning, of course, renders an understanding of meaning-based culture a good fit. Anthropological concepts regarding culture emphasize its immediacy and centrality to activities of daily life and its character as involving an intricate interweaving of connections among activities, persons, values, and technologies that affect meanings for individuals. Clearly these concepts are compatible with psychoanalytic conceptions of the complexity and uniqueness of an individual internal life.

The current shifts in theoretical frame, however, do require the construction of new ideas about some aspects of psychoanalytic thinking. One major area in which revision is necessary is that of psychological health and pathology, since the Oedipus complex is no longer workable and the attempt to impose a taxonomic system such as the *DSM-IV* seems misguided—an effort to be scientific through reducing individual human beings to a list of symptoms. While there is no apparent final consensus in this area, Moore's (1999:134) concept of *optimal participation in construction* offers an interesting possibility. Recall that, as indicated in the introduction, this idea is similar to Gergen's (1994) understanding of psychotherapy as discourse. Further, both Kleinman (1988) and Von Bertalanffy (1968) have noted that severe mental illness involves an inability to participate in a cultural meaning-making process. The ability to participate in a culture and in its creation does not dictate the individual's stance, whether confirming or challenging, toward specific societal conditions. Thus assisting individuals to participate in the culture can be seen as providing those individuals with the requisite means to have an impact on the nature of the cultural surround.

Pat S. was twenty-five when she was admitted to a long-term day hospital. She had been in treatment for a psychotic condition since adolescence and had been on in-patient units several times. Pat had little ability to relate to other patients and often seemed as if she preferred being alone. When she wanted to make contact, she would approach others physically more closely than was usually comfortable for them and announce in a loud voice, "Forewarned is forearmed!" Ordinarily, this resulted in the other person's moving away from her as rapidly as possible; but occasionally, when the other person did not flee, Pat would patiently await a response, although she often was disappointed in the response she got and would then walk away while the other person was talking.

When asked about the reasons for her behavior, Pat indicated that she considered "Forewarned is forearmed" to be the best advice she had ever received and her conveying it to others was her attempt at sharing this wisdom. She told this only to people she thought she might want to have as friends and was disappointed when they did not understand the importance of this message about the need to be vigilant when dealing with the world. She claimed that she was accustomed to this disappointment, however, and did not let it bother her too much. She explained she knew that others in the program had problems in knowing what they should do with their lives, but her problem was much worse—she was having to fight for her very birthright. Her explanation for why this was the case was very difficult to follow, although Pat's anger as she talked about it was quite clear.*

---

*This case was previously presented and discussed in C. Saari, "Intersubjectivity, language, and culture: Bridging the person/environment gap?" *Smith College Studies in Social Work* 69 (1998): 203–220.

Although Pat wanted to have relationships with at least some of the people in her environment, she had difficulty making such relationships and could not participate in the culture around her or in its construction. Although she had some ability to utilize language in a semantic sense, her words did not seem to capture much of her experience in that she could not explain very well why they had so much meaning for her. Certainly she was unable to convey meaning to others in her immediate environment and had little interest in trying to understand the communications of others. Her words did not seem to have linkages either to event representations or to one another so that an explanatory framework could be built. How much she had constructed event representations was not apparent. Yet understanding the culture of Pat's family made it possible to gain an understanding of what Pat herself could convey only in her very global manner.

Pat was an only child whose mother had very much wanted to have children, something very strongly opposed by Mr. S. Mr. S., an intelligent man who was successful in his law practice, nevertheless had some rather paranoid traits and said he did not want to be responsible for bringing a child into a dangerous world only to suffer. Jewish, and having had family members who died in the Holocaust, Mr. S. held fears that were not totally without rationality. An argument about having children had begun shortly after the parents' marriage and had become quite heated. Ostensibly thinking that, once there was a child, her husband would accept the situation and become a good father, Mrs. S. stopped taking birth-control pills and did not tell Mr. S. When Mrs. S. became pregnant and informed her husband, he was furious and insisted that she obtain an abortion. Mrs. S. refused the abortion, and the two became locked into a form of marital warfare in which Mr. S. accused his wife of deception and she countered with charges that he wanted to be a murderer.

Shortly after Pat's birth, Mrs. S. went into a postpartum depression of psychotic proportions and was hospitalized for more than two years. Pat's care in early infancy was, therefore, undertaken by Mr. S. As Mrs. S. had expected, he accommodated his life and his schedule to caring for Pat, not only hiring someone to care for her while he was at work but actually changing his work schedule so that he could spend more time with the child. Mr. S. did, however, indicate that during Pat's early years he had been very busy, working, caring for the child, and visiting his wife. He had little time for socializing with others, and Pat's time was spent either with him or with the housekeeper he had hired. Although Mr. S. spoke with pride about his ability to care for Pat as a baby, he readily acknowledged that he really did not enjoy the work involved and always worried about what fate might befall his daughter. Pat had little interaction with her mother during her infancy because the hospital rules prohibited visits by young children.

Mr. S. remained furious at his wife, not only for her deception in getting pregnant but also for what he saw as her failure to meet her responsibilities to care for him as her husband. By the time Mrs. S. returned to the home, when Pat was two and a half years old, the child was already attached to her father. Indeed, the apparent closeness between Pat and her father continued until Pat's adolescence, at which time she became psychotic.

The relationship between Pat and her mother, already distant and strained, remained so: Pat had difficulty relating to her mother; and for Mrs. S., Pat evoked both guilt over a sense of having failed her and fear over the possibility of her own return to psychosis. In addition, Mr. and Mrs. S. continued their resentment of each other over the issue of having a child.

———

Family life is the first culture in which human beings learn to participate and within which the child is taught how to share in the culture of the community beyond the family. The most important meaning in Pat's family, however, had been constructed prior to her birth, and the dominant theme—whether or not she should have been brought into the world—remained stagnant thereafter. Thus Pat had been excluded from participating in this meaning system. With this information, we understand something about what "Forewarned is forearmed!" and "I have to fight for my birthright" might have meant to her. It must, however, be stressed that this information about Pat's family culture does *not* explain the causes of her mental illness, which should be expected to have complex biopsychosocial roots. It does, however, describe her resulting inability to create meaning for herself and provides a context in which the meaning that she does have can be understood. The deficits prevented Pat from being able to join in the culture around her. As Sullivan (1953) taught, being able to participate in a human community is of major importance to human functioning.

How best to help the Pats of the world is something we have yet to understand fully, but what the information about her tells us is that understanding her environment/culture is critical to understanding her problems in functioning in it. Furthermore, we know that the problems in functioning in society that people with severe mental illness experience are only more exaggerated versions of the kinds of problems that most of us encounter in life. Thus understanding the environment from a perspective that focuses on culture as a meaning system is crucial to understanding a theory for psychotherapy. Bruner (1986), in talking about a new breed of developmental theory on which a theory of psychotherapy could be based, has put it well:

> I think that its central technical concern will be how to create in the young an appreciation of the fact that many worlds are possible, that meaning and reality are created and not discovered, that negotiation is the art of constructing new meanings by which individuals can regulate their relations with each other. It will not, I think, be an image of human development that locates all of the sources of change inside the individual, the solo child. For if we have learned anything from the dark passage in history through which we are now moving it is that man, surely, is not "an island, entire of itself" but a part of the culture that he inherits and then recreates. The power to recreate reality, to reinvent culture, we will come to recognize, is where a theory of development must begin its discussion of mind. (149)

FOUCAULT'S CHALLENGE

IN THE 1960S, social activists, particularly those in the social work profession, criticized psychotherapy, claiming that it only helped the poor and oppressed to adapt to a sick society and thereby participated directly in their oppression. At that time, the formulations regarding the efficacy of therapy often followed Hartmann (1958) and did presuppose an environment to which one should be adapted. Since psychotherapy involved changes in the person and not the environment, it was easy to assume that therapy was inherently endorsing the status quo in society, and it was therefore hard for clinicians to argue with this criticism. Currently, however, such a criticism can readily be dismissed because a postmodern theory of psychotherapy based on the creation of meaning need not rely on a conception of adaptation. A theory of psychotherapy based on concepts of meaning presupposes an environment, but does not presuppose any particular attitude toward or behaviors in that environment. Such a theory needs to assume that psychotherapy can help the person further develop the ability to understand his culture and therefore to participate in it. The healthy person, then, is able to make her own decisions as to what behaviors or attitudes within the environment will best serve her interests.

Postmodern theory does, however, have its own critique of psychotherapy, particularly of psychoanalysis, and this criticism comes in the work of Foucault (1962, 1988, 1990, 1995; Chambon, Irving, and Epstein 1999). Michel Foucault, a French philosopher and social critic, is generally considered to be one of the major figures in postmodern thought. His work involved a detailed examination and discussion of history and social conditions, something he termed *genealogy*, through which he arrived at astonishingly new ideas. In these analyses, Foucault showed that, in Western societies prior to the eighteenth century, social control operated through the external, physical aspects of war and through allegiances to the local lords who engaged in these wars. For the people, this often involved harsh—indeed, brutal—conditions for life since the people had to provide armies and the means to support them.

As the industrial revolution progressed and more people began to live in cities where there was anonymity rather than service to a known local aristocrat, the social structures of feudal arrangements no longer worked. Increasingly, therefore, mechanisms of social control shifted to become individually based and internal rather than external. In these new social arrangements, the individual came to believe that behaving in ways that serve the existing order are natural, proper, and for his or her own benefit. The new power ruled, therefore, not because it hid some major truth through physical repression, but because it produced the "truths" that guided behavior. The fact that people still understand social control as operating through the more repressive methods of earlier times contributes to the efficacy of the new form of power, since it is hidden from sight and examination.

Of the type of power that Foucault described, Wang (1999) says:

One of Foucault's major contributions is his placing of subjectivity in the center of power technology. Power has long been viewed as operating exclusively through the repression of an essential subjectivity. Crushing subjectivity has been assumed as necessary for power to operate. In contrast then to orthodox interpretations of power, Foucault portrays a new form of power, which he suggests is also the most effective mechanism of power. This newly imagined power operates in precisely the opposed direction, not by repressing subjectivity but by promoting, cultivating, and nurturing it. (192)

Power, according to Foucault, is not the threat of death, but the taking over of subjectivity, which gives life meaning—and it is the subjectivity that gives life its meaning that is the concern of psychoanalytic psychotherapy.

The new social order making its debut was, of course, the bourgeois society in which the Protestant work ethic came to hold sway. Thus came the poor laws—the laws regulating public relief—and the belief that those who did not contribute to society economically were not just lazy but also corrupt, godless, and/or perverted. The domination of the new order was enforced through the emergence of institutions designed to discipline those who diverged from socially approved patterns—workhouses, welfare systems, insane asylums, prisons, and the like. Foucault (1995) described in some detail the manner in which these institutions carried out their work through a constant oversight of the body of the individual involved. Nothing could be hidden from the disciplinary power. Yet the oversight of disciplinary power within the society was not merely on the body alone, but also on the mind—the intentions, desires, fantasies, and dreams of the person were suspect and also subject to inspection and control. Foucault saw the new form of power as dominating not just behavior but the total person. Although Foucault did not use this comparison, it might be said that we have all been living in Orwell's 1984 all along.

Foucault regarded the model from which oversight of the whole person could be carried out as that of the Christian confessional. It was not enough that there were sins, but that there were also sinners—and sinners who constantly had to be vigilant to ensure that their behavior, even if outwardly blameless, was not harboring suspect motives underneath. The art form of the novel emerged during this time, and novels were not simply stories of people's lives as outwardly lived, but tales of manners proclaiming that in the end inner goodness would win out over evil. even if the latter were hidden behind money and sophistication. Yet Foucault saw the installation of endless self-analysis not as a cure but as a curse.

It is, of course, not surprising that sexuality as both a hidden and a highly personal and private matter would, in Foucault's mind, become another area in which oversight would have to be crucial. Foucault (1990:35) argues eloquently that sexuality was not repressed, as Freud believed, in Victorian society, but was assigned a status as "secret," thereby ensuring that it would be talked about ad infinitum. As the secret that must be both kept and hidden, sexuality became the metamessage through which people could be reminded of the potential power of their inner desires and of their need to hold those desires in check. In the eighteenth and nineteenth centuries, the necessity of self-restraint in regard to sexuality was, of course, reinforced by fear of syphilis, the disease that would ultimately refuse to remain hidden. Although syphilis is now under control, the same functions may have been played in the twentieth century first by out-of-wedlock pregnancy and more recently by AIDS.

For Foucault (1990), the manner in which sexuality operated as a function of social control was primarily a matter for the middle classes, while the general population was controlled through other means:

> There is little question that one of the primordial forms of class consciousness is the affirmation of the body; at least, this was the case for the bourgeoisie during the eighteenth century. It converted the blue blood of the nobles into a sound organism and a healthy sexuality. One understands why it took such a long time and was so unwilling to acknowledge that other classes had a body and a sex— precisely those classes it was exploiting. The living conditions that were dealt to the proletariat, particularly in the first half of the nineteenth century, show there was anything but concern for its body and sex: it was of little importance whether *those* people lived or died, since their reproduction was something that took care of itself in any case [italics in original]. (126)

Psychoanalysis, for Foucault, became a means of reinforcing social control through a focus on sexuality as well as underscoring its power through sexuality's personal and private character. Freud's patients, as we know, were of the upper or upper-middle class, even if many also were members of a Jewish minority who were often discriminated against. Perhaps that very minority status contributed to the appeal of the talking cure, since it might have exorcised, in some unconscious and mysterious manner, the underlying fault that was brought about by holding such demeaned status and was experienced as central to the person.

Psychotherapy and the professions that practice it, in Foucault's mind, however, also contribute to social control through "normalization," which he saw as even more pernicious than the mere investigation of sexuality. For in the context of the positivist, scientistic times within which Freud lived, not only were inner lives inspected and analyzed, but they were also classified. Thus Freud's vocal adherence to a scientific model of truth meant that it was the technical and, presumably, generalizable aspects of his ideas that he wished to emphasize rather than the more humanistic characteristics of his work, such as according serious attention to the thoughts of even those people who were very troubled and unable to function well. In the process of such normalization, we, in fact, turn people into "cases" and believe we have captured the totality of their existence through a system of diagnostic classifications based on a few behaviors or symptoms. References to "the borderline" and "the schizophrenic," for example, are alive and well in the psychiatric and psychotherapy literature. Foucault also emphasized the fact that prior to the nineteenth century there was homosexual behavior but no homosexuals—that is, there were not people whose sexual behavior was seen as being so fundamental to their being that it was their very identity.

Foucault's criticisms of psychiatry and psychotherapy within the power operations of society predominate within his theory, and he did not offer a formula by which the destructive effects he saw as brought about by mental health practices can be changed. He did, however, allow for the possibility of amelioration of the effects of these practices in that he also had a concept of resistance, even though he did not provide any details about how this might be deployed in combating domination. He did make it clear, however, that true resistance must operate not at a large-scale level, such as a movement for social reform, but at the local level, involving the subjectivity of the individual. Thus Foucault's work, perhaps unintentionally, left open the possibility that psychotherapy *could* operate in a manner that would increase resistance rather than domination. Additionally, Wang (1999) claims that Foucault's ideas focused not so much on the domination of a patient by a therapist through the activity of treatment as on the way in which both of these interacting partners are enveloped and dominated within the broader societal power relationships (managed care readily comes to mind here). Foucault certainly did hope that unmasking the hidden power relationships on which he focused would have positive effects on Western societies as a whole.

CAN WE ANSWER FOUCAULT'S CHALLENGE?

THE DISCUSSION IN this chapter, then, has indicated that a psychotherapy conceived of in postmodern terms can potentially liberate the mentally ill through helping them learn how to participate in their cultural environment. It has, however, also pointed out that psychotherapy can be used as an instrument of domination through its function in creating subjectivities that, in effect, ensure that the person will behave in ways that will perpetuate the power relationships of the existing social order. Understanding the individual's subjectivity as grounded in the construction of self and world through event representations makes both positions comprehensible within the terms of current theories of development and of psychotherapy. How can we know which is true?

The sociologist Steven Seidman (1998) refers to Foucault's theories as naive in the sense that "social life is unimaginable without social norms, identities, and a system of social control. The compelling moral and political issue revolves around the kinds of choices, social differences, and social relations that different systems of social control make possible and the ways they are implicated in democratization and hierarchy" (250). Indeed, Seidman would have us believe that social control in forms other than the "domination" that Foucault discussed is crucial to the very guarantee of continued existence along with others that is essential in any society. Berger and Luckman (1966), in their classic work introducing constructivism into the mainstream of social science thought, gave us this reminder: "*All* social reality is precarious. *All* societies are constructions in the face of chaos [italics in original]" (103). Yet even within these qualifications, Foucault's challenge is a serious one, deserving of answers. Does psychotherapy contribute to domination, or does it liberate?

Many of Freud's early followers had a kind of revolutionary zeal, working with the belief that psychoanalysis, once widely accepted, could alleviate social problems. Altman (1995) points out that Freud himself had a democratic sensibility and that he harbored a kind of liberal political hope that psychoanalysis could ultimately be housed within free public clinics that would treat the poor. The Frankfort school of social critics (Herbert Marcuse, Erich Fromm, Max Horkheimer, and others) combined Freudian and Marxist theories with the hope of thereby conceiving of revolutionary political and social systems that could alleviate the problems of the poor and allow for a truly egalitarian and democratic society. In the United States, Wilhelm Reich believed that sexual repression was responsible for social ills and hoped that dealing with it would lead to a more just society. Unfortunately, although a heritage of alliance between leftist political thought and psychoanalytic theory ought to be valued, none of these theories can be said to have led to their envisioned goals and none are currently in the mainstream of psychoanalytic or psychotherapeutic theory.

Of course, a postmodern answer to the question of whether psychotherapy frees or dominates would say that it does both. In his crosscultural study of healing systems, Kleinman (1988) says: "Healing systems—professional as well as folk—can, though often they do not, offer interpretations that challenge orthodox political definitions of reality" (129). However, arriving at even tentative and very preliminary conclusions about how best, in psychotherapy, to ensure the minimization of aspects of domination, as Foucault conceived of it, requires much further consideration. Even so, we can know that any considerations likely to be truly helpful in this regard will have to take the relationship between the people and their environments very seriously.

PART 2/ DOMINATION OR LIBERATION?

FOUR / INNER LIFE AND THE POSSIBILITY OF FREEDOM

ALTHOUGH IN GENERAL Foucault's work is highly critical of psychoanalysis, he does indicate that "where there is power, there is resistance, and yet . . . this resistance is never in a position of exteriority in relation to power. Should it be said that one is always 'inside' power, there is no escaping it" (1990:95). Foucault, however, never fully explains resistance or how it can be fostered. Nevertheless, if we take seriously Foucault's idea that the form of power that is most commonly exercised in contemporary Western societies is in the creation of subjectivities that continue the existing social organization, it becomes apparent that resistance must take place through subjectivity—through the individual's inner experience of self and the world. Dealing with subjectivity is, of course, specifically what psychotherapy does. Psychotherapy, therefore, is in a particularly critical position either to liberate or to dominate the individual.

Psychotherapy is essentially a process through which a dialogue is used to create, alter, and/or facilitate the client's identity—the personal meaning systems that tell the client who he or she is. Although much of this process has traditionally relied on language for its effectiveness, actually all three of Nelson's (1985) aspects of meaning are involved in the client–therapist interactions. Since psychotherapy involves a relationship with the therapist, a number of interpersonal processes identified in earlier chapters—including self-regulation by another, affect attunement, attachment, social referencing, transitional objects and phenomena, and affect development—can be expected to take place within the therapeutic environment. As is addressed more specifically in part 3, these processes are expected to contribute to the growth of the client's meaning system as treatment occurs.

Current postmodern theorists (Bruner 1986; Gergen 1994; Polkinghorne 1988; Schafer 1992) see identity as occurring in narrative form, as the stories we tell about ourselves or the stories told about us by others.

An understanding that treatment processes involve a dialogue in which this narrated identity is created or reconstructed is compatible with the current social work emphasis on a "strengths perspective" (Saleebey 1992), in the sense that if the therapist relates to the client's pathology, it is likely that what grows in the treatment will be the pathology, whereas if the focus is on healthy aspects of the client's identity, without naively ignoring pathology, then these healthy aspects are what will grow. Maranhao (1990) has explained: "These traits of his identity, however, do not precede dialogue; they are bestowed upon him as he speaks and listens. The subject comes into being together with dialogue and is as much a meaning-content in the process as are the things talked about" (18).

Identity, that basic sense of who we are that guides both our sense of ourselves and our behavior, can be understood to be constituted through dialogue. Identity is not something that fundamentally exists inside an isolated person waiting to be uncovered through an archaeological exploration of the layers of an unconscious. Identity is not something that is formed in some early developmental stage and then endures reasonably intact throughout life. Personal identity is constantly being modified, being created and re-created in negotiations with our interactive partners throughout our entire lives. But as Berger and Luckmann (1966) indicated in their early work on constructivism, "identity remains unintelligible unless it is located in a world" (174). A therapeutic dialogue can be seen to have the express purpose of helping to construct or reconstruct an identity for the client, but this construction must also include that of a world within which the client lives.

In contrast to Erikson's (1963) work on identity as becoming consolidated in adolescence and remaining relatively stable and monolithic thereafter, postmodern theories regard healthy identity as having "multiple voices" (Elliott and Greenberg 1999), being "multifaceted" (Sands 1996; Shawver 1996), or being "complex" (Guidano 1987; Saari 1993). This idea of multiple or complex selves is not unlike that of Mead (1934), who indicated that there are as many selves as there are social roles:

We carry on a whole series of different relationships to different people. We are one thing to one man and another thing to another. There are parts of the self which exist only for the self in relationship to itself. We divide ourselves up in all sorts of different selves with reference to our acquaintances. We discuss politics with one and religion with another. There are all sorts of different selves answering to all sorts of different social reactions. (142)

A healthy identity is presumed to allow the individual to make adaptive behavioral choices in a variety of social contexts. Fennell (1998) has conceptualized healthy identity complexity as having four basic elements: (1) the ability to share meaning with others, (2) the ability to conceive of multiple meanings, (3) the ability to recognize choices for behavior, and (4) the ability to conceive of future possibilities. At a general level, psychotherapy should foster this kind of health along with whatever specific goals the individual brings to it.

The idea of multiple selves has recently had some currency, particularly among relational psychoanalytic theorists who espouse postmodern ideas. In 1996, an entire issue of *Contemporary Psychoanalysis* was devoted to the topic, with contributions from Bromberg (who appears to have been the leading theorist in this area), Davies, Flax, Harris, Lachmann, Pizer, and Slavin. Bromberg (1996) wrote: "I've remarked that 'health is the ability to stand in the spaces between realities without losing any of them—the capacity to feel like one self while being many.' 'Standing in the Spaces' is a shorthand way of describing a person's relative capacity to make room at any given moment for subjective reality that is not readily containable by the self he experiences as 'me' at that moment" (516). In the same article, Bromberg considers the existence of multiple selves to be healthy—the "basis of creativity, playing, illusion, and the use of potential space to further self-growth" (526). However, he sees the multiplicity of selves to be created through intrapsychic processes of dissociation rather than simply through experiences with different environments that evoke and thereby create different aspects of the person. His formulation, therefore, appears to be rooted in a somewhat more pathologically oriented position than is intended here.

The concept of identity complexity takes into account the importance of the environment or culture(s) in which the individual participates. Indeed, the sociocultural surround, with its many different facets and demands, is the reason that complexity is required. Erikson's (1958, 1963, 1969) ideas about the sociocultural influences on personality have long been seen as central to clinical work, as indeed they should be. Yet although his descriptions of the lives of prominent individuals are brilliant in demonstrating the interweaving of personality and the sociocultural surround, there is little in his texts that has a direct bearing on the treatment process. Viewing the environment as an element that is part of the client–therapist dialogue places the social and the cultural in very prominent positions in the treatment process. In the context of post-modernism, however, the treatment dialogue is seen not as uncovering a, probably repressed, TRUTH, but rather as arriving at some of a potentially infinite number of possible truths that might be more adaptive for the client in relation to that individual's life circumstances and goals.

Ideally, therefore, psychotherapy should contribute to the develop-ment of a self that is highly differentiated, articulated, and integrated. Such a self should allow the person to participate in the surrounding cul-ture, but to do so in a way that also permits some reflexivity regarding the relationship between self and environment and therefore some choice regarding behavior within the setting in question.

NORMALIZATION

THE ASPECT OF psychoanalysis that Foucault saw as most harmful was that of "normalization." For Foucault, normalization refers to the creation of norms by which the patient and his behavior, thoughts, or creations can be considered pathological or in need of change. At pres-ent, for example, normalization occurs through the classification of the patient's symptoms as they are arranged in the *DSM-IV*. It is worth not-ing that within psychiatry there is no such thing as a generally accepted profile of health and that all people who venture into a mental health worker's office receive a label defining the particular type of disturbance from which they suffer. These diagnostic labels do not, however, ordi-narily capture the individual's experience very well. Indeed, the use of these labels is promoted, ostensibly by an attempt to make the messy world of human experience and inner life conform to patterns that have been "scientifically observed" in order to arrive at an understanding of the problem and the proper course of treatment. In fact, the linkage between the *DSM-IV* classifications and the properly prescribed treat-ment, particularly treatment through psychotherapy, is rather weak.

The effect of normalization is to undermine clients' confidence in their ability to understand themselves and the world around them, something that Dorpat (1996) has termed "gaslighting," with reference to the well-known Charles Boyer and Ingrid Bergman movie in which a man manipulates the gaslights in his home in order to make his wife believe that she is going crazy. Dorpat believes that many mental health practitioners use covert methods of indoctrination and control without being aware that this is what they are doing. Dorpat points out that both Freud's idea that the therapist must correct the patient's "distorted reality" and the concept of "resistance" have contributed to the practice of methods of indoctrination.

Dorpat (1996) discusses Freud's Wolf Man and Dora cases in order to demonstrate problems that were created by Freud's authoritarian manner in relating to these patients. In his work with Dora, one of the major problems was Freud's failure to take into account the actuality of the adolescent Dora's experience in relation to the sexual overtures of the middle-aged Herr K. and of her father's wish for her to engage in an affair with Herr K. Freud failed to accept the reality of Dora's environment as she saw it, and instead considered her problems to be essentially intrapsychic. This created a treatment environment that contradicted Dora's understanding of what had occurred in her life, an environment from which she fled. Interestingly, Erikson (1962) some time ago noted that Dora returned to see Freud a year after her termination of the treatment, apparently in order to tell him that she had gotten confirmation from Herr K. that events had occurred as she had presented them and not as Freud had claimed. Erikson discusses Dora's need for assurance of her own comprehension of reality as characteristic of adolescence, but this need is actually present throughout the life span.

Interestingly, as the work with Mr. and Mrs. Flynn, discussed in the following case, illustrates, treatment may at least at times be more effective if the focus of the discussion in the clinical hour is on the external reality than if that reality is either dictated or ignored. Due to the connections between external and internal worlds, focusing on the external world is neither less therapeutic nor more superficial than is focusing on the inner world.

Mr. and Mrs. Flynn were a working-class, not particularly psychologically minded couple in their early forties. Their ten-year-old son, Patrick, had been diagnosed as probably having childhood schizophrenia. Although a very bright youngster, Patrick had severe learning difficulties due to an apparent inability to concentrate in class. He could not manage peer relationships and was often a behavior problem in class, where he would distract other children, sometimes by passing strange drawings or notes and other times by severe teasing as well as hitting or stabbing with sharpened pencils. Patrick had an active fantasy life, but one that was disorganized, chaotic, and frequently violent in content. Outside school, Patrick was a loner and an avid reader, usually of science-fiction comic books and *Mad* magazine.

The parents considered Patrick a behavior problem at home because he frequently would not obey their instructions, although he was not usually actively destructive. He had a habit of reading magazines at the dinner table, even though this was expressly forbidden. Patrick seemed to know that this was bothersome to his parents. To them, the *Mad* magazines were (1) a representation of a distorted picture of the world; (2) a statement of his mental problems, about which they felt quite guilty; (3) an accusation that they were also crazy; and (4) an expression of anger and hostility, affects with which they could not deal very well. Although Patrick's problems were fairly severe, a detailed developmental history and testing indicated that he had neurological impairments that probably accounted for much of his pathology. Therefore, while there were problems within the family, they were not the fundamental basis of the pathology.

Upon referral from school authorities, Mr. and Mrs. Flynn sought treatment through a child-guidance clinic. They indicated from the outset that they were quite upset with their son's difficulty, which also made them feel quite ashamed of him. Mr. and Mrs. Flynn were outwardly willing to cooperate with treatment, which, for two years, consisted of weekly appointments for Patrick and weekly appointments with a separate worker for Mr. and Mrs. Flynn. During this time, Patrick's progress was discernable but very slow. His teachers reported improvement, but the parents thought that there had been none at all at home. The parents' therapist also believed that there had been no progress at all in the work with the parents.

During this initial two-year period, Mr. and Mrs. Flynn kept appointments quite regularly and never showed any unwillingness to do so while the clinic thought this necessary for their son. The therapist considered the parents to be quite dependent people who handled any suggestions about how to deal with their son in a highly passive-aggressive manner. Each week, Mr. and Mrs. Flynn would dutifully report on their son's behavior and request help with dealing with it. However, they would then return to point out, without any overt show of anger, that the suggestions had not worked. Over the course of the two years, it also became quite apparent that Patrick was scapegoated within the family. His younger brother, Sean, was openly recognized as being more responsible and competent. Sean was allowed, and at times even actively encouraged, to tease Patrick for mistakes or shortcomings. At other times, it appeared that Mr. and Mrs. Flynn themselves joined in making fun of Patrick's behavior. Mr. and Mrs. Flynn's therapist, whose philosophy about treatment of parents consisted primarily of a simple belief in educational guidance through advice as to how to deal with their children, was extremely frustrated by them and believed that no significant progress was possible.

Following two years of treatment, Mr. and Mrs. Flynn were transferred to me. I quickly saw the Flynns' pattern of presenting problems, openly requesting help, and then demonstrating how this help had been ineffective. However, the Flynns' genuine guilt over what they saw as their own parental failure was also apparent. Therefore, I attempted to divert discussions from just reports on Patrick's behavior to an attempt to learn more about the parents as part of getting to know them as individuals. All along, Mr. and Mrs. Flynn had been cooperative about aspects of what they believed was expected of them, and now, similarly, they were cooperative about offering general information about themselves.

Mr. and Mrs. Flynn had grown up in the same ethnic neighborhood in which they now lived. They had known each other from childhood; in fact, they had lived across the street from each other, but since he was a few years her elder had not played together as children. Both reported their childhoods as being reasonably pleasant and uneventful. Both had graduated from high school with unremarkable records. There was no expectation of further education for either of them. Following high school, Mr. Flynn had spent several years in the service and then returned home to live with his mother and support himself by working as a skilled laborer. His father had died while he was in the service, and he expected to live with his mother until he married. Meanwhile, Mrs. Flynn had graduated from high school and secured a clerical job; she, too, continued to live at home. The two families had always considered each other to be good neighbors, and Mrs. Flynn would occasionally visit with her future mother-in-law, whom she liked, especially after the death of Mr. Flynn's father.

Thus when Mr. Flynn returned from the service, his mother began to invite the future Mrs. Flynn over for dinner. Mr. and Mrs. Flynn considered it quite natural that they should have eventually begun dating and then married. When the house next door to Mrs. Flynn's parents was put up for sale, the Flynns bought it, thus continuing to live on the same block with parents from both sides of the family. This was not an unusual pattern in the neighborhood; in fact, Mr. Flynn had a brother who lived on the next block, and Mrs. Flynn had a sister only a few blocks away.

Both parents reported the marriage to be satisfactory. Indeed, in treatment sessions they presented a somewhat united front in which there appeared to be a genuine affection for each other and a mutually supportive relationship. While Mr. Flynn appeared to get along well with his fellow workers on the job and Mrs. Flynn maintained some contact with girlfriends from high school and her previous work, their primary social contacts were with members of the extended family, again a pattern that neither parent had ever questioned—a natural part of an expectable lifestyle.

Mr. and Mrs. Flynn shared an interest in the maintenance of their modest home, which occupied a large part of their time. They also shared a passion for hockey, and during the hockey season their evenings were always devoted to watching the televised games. Although there was no evidence that either parent ever overindulged, Mr. Flynn would drink a can of beer or two, and Mrs. Flynn would sometimes share in the beer. The two would become very involved in the activity of the game, often yelling invectives or cheering. Both parents considered this activity to be quite normal and their major form of recreation, but Patrick found it somewhat frightening because of the hostility that was expressed and because he seemed to fear that his parents were, or might become, out of control. Although Mr. and Mrs. Flynn recognized that this behavior on their part troubled Patrick, they considered his reaction to be out of proportion since they did little more than yell or occasionally pound a pillow out of frustration. Indeed, it did seem that this recreation was the only time when the Flynns ever allowed themselves to experience or express any anger, with the exception of their battles with Patrick. While the Flynns were not proud of their anger at Patrick, which they knew was expressed in the dinner-table confrontations, they simply could not understand why he did not behave as a "normal" child would and abide by their directive not to read during dinner, which was considered to be a time for family sharing and discussion.

As I encouraged an informal atmosphere in the sessions with the

Flynns and evidenced a noncritical interest in the details of their lives, they began to appear more relaxed. On one occasion, Mr. Flynn asked if I liked hockey, to which I truthfully replied that I did not. Mr. Flynn then said that he bet I did not know anything about the game, and I acknowledged this to be the case. After a long protestation that the public impression about hockey fans was inaccurate—the view that people watched hockey only for the violence of the physical fights that were typical of the game—Mr. Flynn announced that he thought it was a fine game and that I would enjoy it if I knew what was going on. He then directed me to watch a game, saying that he would teach me about it. The following week, Mr. Flynn asked if I had watched a hockey game. I told him that I had, but that I had not understood the rules. I began asking questions, and Mr. and Mrs. Flynn tried to explain the intricacies of the rules, the playing skills, and the performance records of local players. This pattern continued throughout the remainder of the treatment, and to an outside observer parts of sessions would often have sounded like a social discussion of the sport in which the Flynns were the experts and I the learner.

Before long, just before Thanksgiving, Mrs. Flynn mentioned that they had always gone to one of their parents' homes for dinner and had never invited their parents to their house. She thought that it was time they did so, but acknowledged that she was nervous about putting on the dinner. Mr. Flynn indicated he thought it was a fine idea and volunteered to help in the preparations. I shared in the activity through listening to the plans. The dinner worked well, with a few minor hitches that provided for some later mild amusement, and Mr. and Mrs. Flynn were proud of their accomplishment. Later in the treatment, Mrs. Flynn, encouraged by the first success, decided to give a fairly large bridal shower for a member of their extended family. Once again, she was actively supported by her husband. The event proved to be a total success.

Apparently encouraged by his wife's new successes, Mr. Flynn decided to undertake some major remodeling inside the house. Thus the sessions also included discussions of his work, his plans, and her participation with him, especially in projects involving sewing—new curtains or new slipcovers. Problems encountered in the work were discussed, with each parent offering suggestions to the other about different ways of trying to solve them. On occasion, I shared an observation or two about possibilities, but served primarily as an interested and encouraging listener. Over the course of time, this discussion took place about most of the rooms of the house.

The last room to be remodeled was the master bedroom. During this project, Mr. and Mrs. Flynn came to one session with a markedly different demeanor than was typical for them. They were clearly angry with each other and reported that they had been engaging in a major argument—the first such they could remember. Mrs. Flynn wanted to buy a new queen-size bed, and Mr. Flynn was opposed to the idea. Both were very angry and hurt, and neither could understand the other's position. The difficulty was that neither had been able to discuss openly the reasons behind their positions. Mr. Flynn finally was able to admit that he was hurt because he assumed this meant his wife wanted to get more distance from him during the night. He said he liked sleeping with her, enjoyed feeling her body next to his, did not want this to change, and did not like to think that she wanted such a change. Mrs. Flynn was clearly shocked that this had been his assumption. She, shyly and with some embarrassment, indicated that she liked having sex with her husband and had been thoroughly enjoying some fantasies about what fun they could have together in a larger bed. Both indicated that they had never before really discussed their feelings about their sexual relationship with each other.

My work with the Flynns occurred over a two-year period. During this time, there were also discussions about Patrick's behavior and progress. However, increasingly the nature of these discussions changed from the parents reporting problems and expecting me to provide solutions to a process in which they would engage in problem solving in relation to Patrick in the same manner as the discussions about planning family events and remodeling the house. In these discussions, they seemed far less concerned about doing the "right" thing. They became much more relaxed about Patrick's reading at the table, although they did not like it, and finally reported that they had directly told Patrick that he could read if he wanted, but that they wished he would not since it excluded him from the family discussions. For a time, Patrick did continue his reading, but the parents tolerated it, and eventually he stopped. Gradually, Mr. and Mrs. Flynn's relationship with Patrick changed, and they no longer allowed Sean to tease him in their presence.

Patrick continued to have serious difficulties, but his improvement was marked. He continued to need special help at school, but was doing well within this structure. Mr. and Mrs. Flynn seemed much more comfortable with the idea that their son had limitations and would probably always have trouble of some sort. They no longer saw this as evidence that they were bad parents, however, and they were more freely engaged in cooperating with the school. At this point, active treatment was terminated with the understanding that in all probability Patrick would need further help in the future, but that at least he was making as much progress as could be expected. In the process of terminating, Mr. Flynn said that he thought the main thing he had learned was that as a parent one has choices over how to handle situations and that one had to think about how best to deal with them. I had never verbalized this principle to them.*

———————

The major problem for the Flynns was their experience of Patrick's problems as meaning that they were inadequate parents. They thus experienced their families as being critical of them, and their initial contacts in the mental health center were simply an extension of that experience. Their passive-aggressive stance with the first therapist actually constituted a protest that they were not to blame. The shift to allowing the Flynns to teach me about hockey gave them the experience of being recognized as competent experts and as people who had a right to feel anger. Once the Flynns had been able to receive some validation for their competence in one area, they used the therapeutic experience to expand their sense of competence into other important areas of their lives. They were able to grow into being mature adults who could be both sexual and adequate parents. It is important to note that the arenas through which the Flynns developed their sense of competence (holiday dinners, more renovations, and the like) were chosen by the Flynns themselves— not by me.

Mr. Flynn's statement during the termination process that he had learned that parents had choices about how to deal with their children is particularly interesting because this treatment occurred and was recorded long before I had any thoughts about identity complexity. It serves as a good example of the manner in which a shared focus on the external world in treatment can have very effective results. While some

———————

*This case was previously presented and discussed from a different perspective in C. Saari, *Clinical social work treatment: How does it work?* (New York: Gardner Press, 1986).

theorists might discount the treatment with the Flynns as not being true psychotherapy but rather parent counseling, I prefer to think that parent counseling is one area in which treatment has sometimes been particularly effective because therapists themselves have traditionally had more freedom from classical dictates to focus exclusively on the intrapsychic.

My work with Mr. and Mrs. Flynn also focused on calling to their attention and expanding their strengths rather than on treating pathology or shortcomings.

REPRESSION AND THE EFFECTS OF DOMINATION

THE REPRESSION OF affects or knowledge was a centerpiece of Freud's theory of the mind and one that guaranteed him a position of strength within the therapy. If one granted the existence of the unconscious as well as that Freud was an expert in uncovering repressed material, one had essentially given up the possibility of disagreeing with him convincingly—that which is in one's unconscious mind is by definition something about which one has no awareness. As Siegel (1999) has pointed out, however, Freud's conception of a stimulus barrier that protects the child from overwhelming anxiety in early childhood is simply no longer accepted; instead, "the brain can be called an 'anticipation machine,' constantly scanning the environment and trying to determine what will come next" (30). In accord with current neurobiological information, psychoanalytic theory has needed to change its understanding of the unconscious, considering the unconscious to be the infinite ways in which knowledge can potentially be constructed.

Describing memory, Siegel (1999) writes:

This reconstruction process may be profoundly influenced by the present environment, the questioning context itself, and other factors, such as current emotions and our perception of the expectations of those listening to the response. Memory is not a static thing, but an active set of processes. Even the most "concrete" experiences, such as recalling an architectural structure, are actually dynamic representational processes. Remembering is not merely the reactivation of an old engram; *it is the construction of a new neural net profile with features of the old engram and elements of memory from other experiences, as well as influences from the present state of mind* [italics in original]. (28)

There is, however, a kind of unconscious memory that is active from birth and is usually referred to as "implicit" memory. When implicit memory is activated, the person is not aware of remembering anything, but the current thought, condition, or event is eliciting some aspect of previous experience in a way that colors the current thought or situation. Clinicians are, of course, very well acquainted with the operation of implicit memory in anniversary reactions and action patterns that take place without conscious intent. A few years ago, a rather disturbed woman who believed that she had been seriously abused in her childhood was walking around my office, which she often did when she was very anxious. She picked up an opaque pitcher to admire it, not knowing that I used this pitcher to water flowers and that it did at that time have some water in it. Her actions occurred so fast that I did not have time to warn her of this. When some of the water spilled, she automatically jerked her body away from me, flinching as if she expected that I would strike her. Implicit memory guides such behavior.

On the basis of my client's behavior with the pitcher, it can be assumed that this client has, at some time in her life, experienced some physical abuse and probably some abuse that occurred more than once. It does not, however, warrant the conclusion that this client's (explicit) recollections of childhood abuse were literally true. Memories of such events occur within "explicit" memory, which is understood to be different from implicit memory. Explicit memory can easily be influenced by the circumstances surrounding retrieval. Additionally, explicit memory is not "immaculate" in the manner that Freud believed—that is, it is not an exact recording of what happened (Schimek 1975). Perceptual biases operating at the time of an event or ignorance of some of the facets of the event mean that what we remember is often inaccurate. But if the event is in some manner traumatic for the person, it is possible that neural processes may be frozen and unable to record the event. It is important, therefore, for a psychotherapist to be very cautious about implying that a client's memory is accurate without external verification of the event. Relying on Freud's conceptions of repression and the accuracy of perception can lead to serious problems.

What has been referred to as "recovered-memory therapy" is an example of the manner in which psychotherapy can amount to domination of the client, with quite seriously damaging results. This type of therapeutic fad appears to be waning, but it was extensively practiced from the late 1980s until the mid-1990s when a number of former patients of recovered-memory therapy began winning large amounts of money for reparation of damages by their therapists, some of whom lost their licenses to practice. While the example of recovered-memory therapy as a form of domination is a useful one for illustrating the problems of which Foucault warned, it should be understood that most of what he was describing is far more subtle than this.

Ms. Y (a generalized, not a real-life, client) seeks treatment for a depression (or an anxiety or other unpleasant states) that includes difficulty sleeping (or headaches, low self-esteem, difficulty in intimate relationships, or a host of other possible symptoms). As a part of the intake interview, Dr. X includes the question as to whether the client has ever been sexually abused. Ms. Y says this did not occur. Dr. X then asks, "Are you *sure?*" Ms. Y says yes, but wonders why Dr. X put so much emphasis on this. A little later in the treatment, Ms. Y relates a particularly unpleasant dream (or a host of other specific behaviors or experiences). Now Dr. X again asks if Ms. Y is sure she was not abused, saying that many of the patients she has seen who have the same problems as Ms. Y have been sexually abused. Ms. Y again denies having had such an experience, and Dr. X says, well, if anything Ms. Y remembers seems to hint at abuse as a possibility, she should report it in the therapy because remembering the abuse can be very helpful. The human mind is very creative, and depressed patients are often desperate to get well, so a little later Ms. Y tentatively reports some experience, dream, or memory that might have some relationship to sexual abuse. Now Dr. X becomes very actively interested in the report, asking for more detail and, in the process of asking what more the client remembers, suggesting that what Ms. Y has remembered must be true and that more might have gone on than the patient has remembered so far.

Once the client has raised the possibility of a memory, Dr. X focuses almost entirely on recovering more memories, and the therapy becomes a long search for the details of what Ms. Y, now labeled by her therapist as a courageous survivor, has had to endure. The number of incidents of abuse, their savage detail, and the number of "perpetrators" multiplies, sometimes even including "satanic ritual abuse" (external evidence of which has never been found) because it is understood that if Ms. Y is not yet feeling better, then there must be more to be remembered.

Ms. Y is also encouraged to think about a confrontation with the perpetrator(s), an act that is said to confirm the strength she has gotten through the therapy. Ms. Y is also told that since perpetrators always lie, the confrontation is not about negotiating with them or trying to understand their perspectives, but about helping her to "focus her anger," which will allow her to understand that what happened to her was not her fault, thereby increasing her self-esteem. Ms. Y is, therefore, told that she must not engage in any interaction with the perpetrator beyond the confrontation itself—at least not at that time. When Ms. Y does confront someone, usually her father or another close family member, and that person denies that the abuse occurred, she is told that the perpetrator is "toxic" to her health and that she must now cut off all relations with that person until the abuse is acknowledged.

This example may seem extreme to people who have not had experience of recovered-memory therapy or its therapists; however, there have been many very popular self-help books and many educational events for professionals regarding this therapy. The most influential book has been *The Courage to Heal,* written by Ellen Bass and Laura Davis, who are not therapists by professional training, but who nevertheless have had considerable influence over some professionals. In the first edition of the book, Bass and Davis (1988) said, "So far, no one we've talked to thought she might have been abused, and then later discovered that she hadn't been. The progression always goes the other way, from suspicion to confirmation. If you think you were abused and your life shows the symptoms, then you were" (15). Although Bass and Davis modified this statement, and some others, in the third edition of their book, the work continues to be supportive of recovered-memory therapy and to offer exercises to those who want to work on remembering.

Is Ms. Y better as a result of her therapy? The chances are that she is not, that she and her therapist have discovered that her abuse was monstrous, and that it will take many years for her to get well. Meanwhile, the abuse and her anger over it have become a central part of her life, she has alienated her family and others in her support group, and she has become increasingly more dependent on her therapist. Goldberg (1997) has referred to the practices of some of the recovered-memory therapists as being similar to those used by cult leaders. Dorpat (1996), while not referring to therapists who use this kind of treatment, has also discussed some psychotherapy practices as being cult-like.

What is paradoxical about the recovered-memory-therapy movement is that it arose out of feminists' legitimate concerns about Freud's sexist attitudes toward women and the lack of attention given to the serious problem of child abuse. Foucault believed the problem was not that the therapist had power while the client did not; rather, he said, both are influenced by power—there is no escaping it (Wang 1999). While it is possible for psychotherapy to be freeing, it is likely to be dominating when the therapist uses it as a tool for the rectification of specific political or cultural problems—even if those problems are real and the stated aim of the reparation is legitimate. This is true not only for recovered-memory therapy, but for other types of treatment as well.

Therapists are ordinarily experts on possible ways to think about the personal experiences of the patient, but they are *not* experts on clients' experiences. When they make claims to this expertise, the treatment is likely to be dominating rather than freeing.

U NDERSTANDING WHETHER THE result of psychotherapy contributes to the domination or the liberation of the individual
requires an understanding of the psychological effects of interactions between person and environment. There are, of course, so many
variables that can contribute to an analysis of these interactions that
achieving any certainty about causes in this relationship has been and
will continue to be all but impossible. Yet, conceding that proof is not
possible, more information about this is available than theories of psychotherapy have taken into account to date. Bronfenbrenner's ecological formulations provide some interesting guidelines. For example, he
said:

> Developmental effects are not likely to be manifested until the per-
> son moves from his present primary setting into another, potential
> primary setting, that is, from a setting that has instigated and cur-
> rently maintains the person's present level and direction of func-
> tioning to another setting requiring the person to take initiative to
> find new sources of stimulation and support. Such transition
> between two primary settings is called a *primary transition*. Sleeper
> effects of earlier primary settings are most likely to be observed
> after primary transitions have taken place, since these are usually
> separated in time by months or years. (1979:286)

Thus major transitions in a person's life are times when problems that
developed in earlier settings but were not evident in the previous settings
may become apparent. From this perspective, for example, the young
child's difficulty in entering school might be seen as involving a fear of
losing a sense of self in the unknown school environment. Current theory about school phobia places emphasis on separation anxiety, and
clinical experience seems to support this interpretation. However, the

loss of the caretaker may not rest in a fear of psychic separation, but in a fear of having to cope with a world that has been characterized as dangerous—dangerous, that is, without the assistance of the information available from social referencing provided by the caretaker.

Defining mental health as identity complexity means that being able to maintain a coherent sense of self while moving between different environments is one indicator of healthy functioning. Clients' ability or inability to move from one environment to another with relative ease can often be observed in psychotherapy.

Blanche (a pseudonym that seems appropriate because of certain similarities to Blanche DuBois in *A Streetcar Named Desire*) had grown up in a small town in the American South. The family, part of the local aristocracy, resided in a large old mansion that, along with extensive land holdings farmed by tenants, had been inherited by her mother. It was, in fact, the income from the tenants that provided the family living—a quite meager one for the lifestyle to which they both aspired and pretended. Blanche's father had grown up in a tenant shack in another town, but before his marriage had worked his way through college. At one time, he had been the principal of the local high school, but he left that position, ostensibly because of a disagreement with the local school board in which he felt his values were being violated and he could not compromise. Blanche, however, suspected that the real truth was that her father was incompetent.

During most of Blanche's life, her father did not work; he played the role of the local intellectual, spending much time in his study (although Blanche claimed that he had not read most of his impressive-looking books). In his walks through the town, Blanche's father carried candy in his pockets to disperse to the children who crowded around him. Blanche noted that she never got any of it. Meanwhile, she claimed, she had to make do with clothes that were made over to look new—a skill at which her mother became quite adept. Thus Blanche's image of her father was of a man who was a total sham in almost all aspects of his life. She could, however, convey a picture of what her father was like, whereas her descriptions of her mother were much more vague. The mother seemed to have remained the long-suffering but quiet aristocrat—the one who really managed the family affairs, but from the background and in a manner that was competent but emotionally distant from her two daughters, of whom Blanche was the junior by about two years.

In high school, Blanche began to see her role in life as being to expose the hypocrisy of not only her own family life but also that of the entire conservative and religious culture of the small town. Her behavior evoked much disapproval from her father, but Blanche seemed to enjoy their angry confrontations, which were also somewhat sexualized and gave her a sense of her own boundaries. Her mother apparently remained silent and apart from the frays. Blanche began drinking and flirting openly with any male in proximity. She noted that no one in the town would have believed that, in fact, she was a virgin on her wedding night; furthermore, she did not want them to believe such a thing. When she left home for college, she wrote detailed letters about often fictitious escapades to supposed friends whom she knew would repeat the tales. In actuality. she was a good student, majoring in literature since she loved fiction. Following graduation she returned home, not knowing where else to go, and taught for two years, but she found life dull because there was little left for her to do to shock the community. Thus, although she was very frightened by the prospect, she convinced her older and more conventional sister that they should move to the sin capital of the country—New York City.

Once in the city, both sisters obtained employment and began a life in which they met a variety of young men, attended many parties, and consumed a good deal of alcohol. Blanche often wrote home embellished letters about their wild existence. However, before long her sister, having become seriously involved with a young man, decided to marry. This turn of events threatened to leave Blanche alone, but she received a proposal of marriage from the best friend of her sister's fiancé. She did not care much about him, but he had certain advantages: he was reasonably reliable, wealthy—and Jewish, which would surely make for talk back home. Although Blanche claimed that she never really thought the marriage would last very long—and, indeed, there were problems from the beginning—she soon decided that she would like to have the experience of motherhood. The result was a son, Robb.

Blanche found that being a mother was a wonderful experience, and she became extremely invested in her son, a situation that made the marriage worse since her husband complained loudly of her relative lack of attention to him. In spite of the unsatisfactory marriage,

Blanche decided that Robb should not go through life as an only child so she managed a second pregnancy, which resulted in a daughter. Shortly after this pregnancy, Blanche asked her husband to leave, which he did, though continuing to meet all her financial demands and maintaining contact with both her and the children. Now basically alone in a city of which she was still very afraid, Blanche considered returning to her hometown; however, not wanting her children to grow up with the kind of hypocrisy she thought herself to have experienced as a child, and not wanting them to have to cope with the negative reputation she had purposely built for herself there, she remained in New York.

Other than her activities with her children, and despite a small circle of friends, life for Blanche became relatively bleak and isolated. She had at least one opportunity to remarry, but she had no desire to do so. She described herself as the type of person who could get along beautifully with the doorman and the grocer, but simply could not manage anything more intimate. She spent much time alone and became increasingly depressed, a condition for which she ultimately sought psychoanalysis. Treatment lasted for several years, and Blanche thought of it as being quite helpful in some ways. However, she concealed from her analyst that she had become alcoholic, invariably being quite inebriated in the late evening. When she eventually did reveal this, along with her inability and reluctance to change it, there came an agreement to end the therapy with the idea that all that could be achieved had been accomplished.

Blanche continued to be invested in her children, especially Robb, who was very responsive to her reading bedtime stories to him. Separations, such as the beginning of school, were difficult, but they were managed with the help of her analyst. Thus the children grew to be intellectual achievers and were seemingly well adjusted. Blanche attempted to protect them from her periodic attacks of irrational rage and her alcoholism by having her former husband buy for her the apartment next to hers. She had a door made in the wall between the two kitchens and declared that the children were to live in one while she lived in the other. The children were forbidden to enter her quarters except at certain times, and she similarly gave them privacy. However, in the late evenings following considerable alcohol consumption, Blanche would have difficulty retaining her resolve and her boundaries. Thus she established a pattern of going to her son's bedroom in an inebriated condition. She would sit on his bed, and the two would engage in long intellectual discussions. This continued throughout his adolescence in spite of her recognition that it was not good for him.

Robb experienced very serious psychiatric difficulties after leaving home for college and was eventually admitted to a long-term inpatient unit. At the request of the hospital, Blanche presented herself for treatment, although claiming that she was terrified of venturing out alone in the sinful city. She quickly pointed out that she herself was beyond reclamation and, furthermore, had no desire to change, even though she had become a virtual prisoner in her own apartment; however, she was willing to do whatever was required to help Robb. Thus she agreed to attend the necessary weekly appointments with me, and I agreed to work with her regarding Robb's problems, but not hers. She admitted that she "fortified" herself against the terrors of the trip to the hospital, but kept her appointments regularly in relatively sober condition.

During his hospitalization, Robb frequently attacked Blanche for her problems, laying at her feet the responsibility for his difficulties. With my support, Blanche was able to maintain a position that, while she knew she had been far from a perfect mother, she had done the best she could. When Robb would aver that he could not get better unless she changed, she would tell him that her life was basically over, that he had his life yet to live, and that he would have to live it for himself independently of whatever she did. She used her sessions with me to deal with her guilt over her failings and her sadness in seeing the seriousness of Robb's problems and the pain he was having to endure.

Initially, Blanche protested that parents' group meetings, which were required, were not for her. She noted that at the time she had terminated analysis, group therapy had been considered, but that her analyst told her she was not a good candidate for it since it would only give her an opportunity to act out her not inconsiderable tendency to be exhibitionistic. Indeed. this tendency was apparent from the outset. Blanche would, for example, arrive for her individual appointments flamboyantly dressed and would greet me with a dramatic hug and kiss in the waiting room, quickly glancing around to see what effect this would have on me as well any others who happened to be present. When alone with me, this seductive behavior was replaced by a very serious demeanor, and for this reason I never challenged her more public behavior, which after a time did stop.

With some reluctance, Blanche joined the parents' group (it was led by someone other than me), and she caused quite a stir at the initial session. Fairly quickly, however, she was impressed that she had achieved acceptance in the group in spite of her provocative behavior, became an active participant in discussions, and began expressing to me her feelings of sympathy for the other parents and their problems with their children. She proudly referred to them as "my family group" and began to talk of long-neglected memories of a variety of distant relatives and family friends who had often been in and out of her childhood home. She recalled that while the Southern culture had indeed been a sham in many respects, there had also been a certain quality of warmth and sharing in the small town. At Christmastime, Blanche spent several days making brandied peaches according to a recipe she recalled from her childhood and proudly presented each parent and me with a jar as a gift. She noted that this was the first time in years that she had felt as if she had some truly meaningful work to do.

During this time, Blanche's drinking did not decrease significantly; however, on the relatively few occasions when Robb was at home, she did manage to avoid going to his room at night. These home visits were apt to be stormy, and Blanche, who had managed to acquire my home telephone number from the public directory, developed a habit of calling me in the middle of the night instead of going to Robb's room. While the brief discussions on the telephone were not useful in terms of content, they did assist her in maintaining her intent not to invade her son's privacy.

On one weekend evening, Blanche called me when I happened to be having a party. Hearing the background noise over the phone, Blanche inquired if there was a party going on. Told that there was, Blanche seemed surprised and then asked, "Have you been drinking?" Not sure how to handle this, but concerned that the truth might be evident, I answered yes. Blanche indicated that under the circumstances she would prefer not to keep me on the telephone and hung up. At her next appointment, Blanche said she had been surprised because she had not pictured me as "the life-of-the-party type," but she said little more about the incident. However, at her session two weeks later she proudly announced that she had joined Alcoholics Anonymous, had been attending meetings almost nightly, and had decided to try to stop drinking—at least, to drink less than she had been doing. This, she announced, was for herself, not her son. She then also pointed out that she had been impressed with my honesty on the night of the party, saying she assumed that the incident must have been a little embarrassing to me since such behavior was not supposed to be part of a therapeutic and professional image. She indicated it must have taken courage to admit the truth, but she thought that if I could deal with being truthful and face the consequences, then she guessed she could learn to do it too.

Subsequently, Blanche continued to attend AA meetings regularly and to cut down on her drinking. She began talking more and more about her need for others in her life now that both of her children were grown. She made a trip to her hometown and found that she still had some friends there; had enjoyed attending church services, which she had not done for years; and had made contact with the AA organization there. Thus within a few months, she had made arrangements to return home to the environment in which her life could have some meaning. For a time after her move, Blanche kept in touch with me, indicating that she still occasionally went on "binges," but that for most of the time she was sober, was occupying herself with keeping up her house and attending church and AA activities, and had found life in general to be far more satisfying than it had been for her in many years.*

Blanche had constructed the entire meaning of her life in the context of her hometown. She could not move her sense of self from one setting to another: once she left home, she did not have a good sense of who she was or what the meaning of her life might be. The loss of her sister through marriage may have been very significant in that the sister served as someone with whom she could share impressions of the New York environment. Alone, Blanche had failed to be able to abstract a coherent sense of self from her environment, something that in Nelson's (1985) tripartite theory of meaning would indicate a deficit in the development of the cognitive skills that underlie categorization. Thus Blanche's identity remained insufficiently differentiated from the environment in which she had initially constructed her world. (Note also that Robb's problems similarly became evident after his move from home to a university.)

---

*This case was previously presented and discussed in C. Saari, *Clinical social work treatment: How does it work?* (New York: Gardner Press, 1986).

We cannot definitively say what characteristics of Blanche's early life left her with insufficient internal resources to move to a new environment. However, using Werner and Kaplan's (1963) theory, we can say that the cognitive ability to construct a sense of self comes from the sharing of perceptions of the external world with a significant other. On that basis, we can speculate that there were insufficient opportunities to share her experiences directly with significant others in her home environment. This seems to fit with a Winnicottian (1965a) perspective in which Blanche could be considered as having an overdeveloped false self and little contact with her true self. In that theory, a false self develops out of a situation in which either the child learns to put her caretaker's needs before her own or the caretaker impinges on the child's true self through too much intrusion into the child's inner world so that the child needs a false self to deflect unwanted intrusions away from the true self. Further, I suspect that Blanche experienced herself as being as much a "sham" as she considered her father to be, although I cannot recall her ever having specifically said this.

The factors that apparently allowed Blanche to make changes in her life, including the decision to move back to her hometown, are more apparent. Blanche did love her son, and his difficulties did serve as a genuinely motivating force evoking considerable, very real emotion in her. She did not experience Robb, her "family group," or me as being "shams"; indeed, she was in a situation in which the sharing of emotions with others who became significant to her apparently enabled her to get into much better contact with her long-submerged true self. From a traditional clinical perspective, there are a number of reasons to say that the work with Blanche was successful: she was able to stop her intrusions into Robb's bedroom and his life in general; she was able to make steps toward sobriety; and she was able to stop thinking of herself and her life as beyond reclamation.

Did the therapy contribute to Blanche's domination, or was it freeing? After all, as a result of the therapy, Blanche decided to return to an environment that she herself had seen as problematic for her. It might be argued that this was a defeat for Blanche in that it was an admission that she could not function elsewhere. Yet the evidence is that Blanche experienced her return as a relief. Knowing that identity must be constructed in the context of an environment helps in understanding this. A return to the primary environment may be necessary for a person to have the opportunity to resume the process of construction of a self that has been incomplete. Utilizing Foucault's theory, Wang (1999) indicates that "the search for one's own claim to identity directly challenges the current practices of knowledge formation" (201). In other words, the construction of a personal identity, presumably one that is not totally embedded in the environment in which it was formed, is a form of resistance.

Making what Bronfenbrenner (1979) would call a "primary transition" is a common event in young adulthood, and the ability to abstract a sense of self that can remain intact in a different environment may well be similar to what Erikson (1964) thought of as a process of "identity consolidation" in adolescence. For some young adults, like Blanche, the departure from the environment of the family of origin may be experienced as an escape, but this does not necessarily mean that the transition will fail. For example, in a study of gay men who had been able to achieve a positive gay identity, Dooley (1998) found that commonly the men had found it necessary to make a geographic move in order to develop the positive identity. A successful move to a new setting is a major psychological achievement, since it contributes to an ability I have called "transcontextualizing." This is the psychological ability to imagine the experience of the self in different environments and is an important aspect of identity complexity.

CONDITIONS THAT FACILITATE THE ABILITY TO CREATE MEANING

THE ABILITY TO transcontextualize is dependent on the ability to create and maintain the meaning system that we call identity. Thus Blanche's ability to create and maintain an identity that could be both solid and flexible enough to allow her to transcontextualize, to maintain a sense of who she was in New York, had not developed sufficiently. Her return to her Southern roots, therefore, can be seen as her attempt to reexperience herself within her primary environment in order to develop further her ability to create meaning. The creation of meaning, however, is not an individual, intrapsychic achievement, but an interpersonal, intersubjective activity, and it was Blanche's experience with me and her "family group" that gave her both the opportunity to engage with others in meaning making and the incentive to increase her satisfaction with her life. Such an experience should be understood not as the result of interpretation, but as the awakening of inherent healthy potential in an environment that is facilitating.

Ultimately, this treatment experience allowed Blanche the confidence to return to her primary environment under conditions in which there was at least the potential for her to resume constructing a sense of self that would not have to be captive to the aspects of that environment that felt foreign to her. The subjectivity that was created in her treatment, therefore, did not dominate but liberated her. Foucault posited that human beings are dominated through the creation of subjectivities that perpetuate conservative distributions of power. The claim here is that a psychotherapy that takes the environment seriously can liberate the individual from the domination of conservative power arrangements through the encouragement of affective/cognitive capabilities that allow for some psychological distance from the immediate environment and therefore the ability to transcontextualize.

At least five aspects of affective/cognitive activities are important for the ability to engage in the creation of meaning and are developed, practiced, and maintained in interpersonal interactions:

1. The individual must be able to maintain a sense of self as different from but related to the interactive partner. As Winnicott (1965b) indicated, it is not possible for human beings to be able to retain a sense of self when either fused with or isolated from other humans. Therefore, when interacting with an other, the individual constantly modulates the emotional or *interpsychic space* between them in order to maintain optimal conditions for the creation and maintenance of identity (Saari 1986, 1991). Winnicott (1975a) observed that anger creates distance and boundaries between people, while love or affection pulls individuals closer.

2. The continuation of interpersonal communication, including the individual's incentive to maintain or terminate the communication, is determined through affective/cognitive activity, as can be seen in the example of the self-regulating other (Stern 1985). Not only may one partner be aware of some dimensions of the interactive partner's inner experience, but each partner's inner experience may also be altered out of resonance with the affective state of the other. This is, therefore, a mutual rather than an individual process.

3. There is also a relationship between the nature and intensity of

affective/cognitive activity and the relative degree of experienced organization of the self (Krystal 1988). Experiencing strong affect frequently becomes a focus around which an individual can maintain a sense of organization. For example, anger or a negative affect can help someone under stress continue to function, at least for a time. However, affect that is very intense and of lengthy duration usually becomes disorganizing.

4. The ability to tolerate strong affect without becoming disorganized varies greatly from one person to another, with the difference related to experiences of affect attunement that have occurred previously (Zetzel 1970). Affective/cognitive activity also serves an evaluative function, assessing both the relative pleasure or pain level of the individual and the particular situation (Basch 1976). Thus affective/cognitive activity indicates not only self-esteem but also the degree of safety in the environment, as in Freud's (1920) concept of signal anxiety. This evaluative activity probably begins and is encouraged through social referencing (Emde 1989).

5. Finally, affective/cognitive activities can provide the individual with vitality from a sense of participation in a human community or a depression from a sense of exclusion from that community. This is in accordance with Sullivan's (1953) idea of consensual validation and Seton's (1981) idea that people like to experience strong emotions because it makes them feel human. This sense of vitality can be important in providing motivation for continuing the process of creating meaning and identity.

These five aspects of affective/cognitive functioning interacting together on a moment-to-moment basis can account for fluctuations in a person's ability to process experience. But if any of them are stunted due either to deficits in early experience or to subsequent trauma, the person may have a long-term inability to utilize the presence of another person for creating meaning, in general, and to transcontextualize, in particular.

Although the availability of another human being is a necessary condition if the capacity to create meaning is to become highly developed, that availability in itself does not constitute a sufficient condition. Indeed, throughout life a number of other factors affect this capacity and the likelihood of its functioning well. These include but are undoubtedly not limited to the following:

1. Physical energy must be available. The person's creation of meaning will be facilitated if he or she is in good health, is in a rested state, and has an ability to devote attention to creating meaning rather than to another bodily activity. Clearly, problems in neurological functioning can affect meaning-making activity. The use of alcohol or other drugs can also negatively influence the ability to create meaning.

2. The individual's internal state must be experienced as sufficiently stable. There must not be so much intrapsychic conflict that it debilitates the person. However, some degree of conflict can motivate the person to create meaning in order to solve the problems involved.

3. The environment must be experienced as both physically and emotionally safe. If the person must devote energy to remaining alert to potential danger or injury, that will detract from his freedom to create meaning and from the energy available for that work.

4. A history of reasonably attuned human relationships will make the person more likely to be able to engage productively in meaning making, because the individual's capacity to create meaning develops over time and, once developed, can endure some adverse conditions.

5. The specific content of the individual's picture of self and of the world—for example, whether they are seen as good, bad, helpful, or evil—will either encourage or depress the capacity to create meaning.

6. The individual must understand the wider cultural environment, feel comfortable within it, and expect others in that culture to be sympathetic to her emotions and actions.

There are, of course, degrees of severity in negative conditions for constructing meaning, with extremes causing trauma, of which Moore (1999) says: "The traumatized person lacks the ability, the opportunity, or both to initiate, create, or integrate this interaction. Potential reality overflows the capacity to construct it, and the result is not a reality created by one's experience, but a loss of one's capacity to participate in it at all" (168).

The environmental conditions that facilitate or inhibit the ability to create meaning are of course essentially the same whether the environment in question is that of the therapy room or of the world outside.

THE EFFECTS OF POVERTY AND DISCRIMINATION

BOLGER AND CO-WORKERS (1995:1107) observed that in 1992, children were the poorest age group in the United States, with 21.9 percent under the age of eighteen living below the federally designated poverty level. McLoyd (1998:185) noted that over a period of nearly two decades, the level of economic deprivation associated with childhood poverty had increased, with 32 percent of all poor children from ages zero to five years having families 50 percent below the poverty threshold in 1975, but 47 percent of such children having families below that level in 1993. For African-American children, the picture is even bleaker: Corcoran and Adams (1997) found that "black children were five times more likely to be poor and eight times more likely to be persistently poor during childhood than white children were" (515). There is a serious problem here, the significance of which is further highlighted by the fact that several studies have shown that children are at particular risk for not completing high school and for continuing to live in poverty when their parents' income is persistently below the poverty level during their preschool years (Burchinal et al. 1997; McLoyd 1998).

Several studies of the effects of poverty on children point out that much of the influence occurs indirectly through effects on parents (Duncan and Brooks-Gunn 1997). Brooks-Gunn, Duncan, and Maritato (1997) indicate that such indirect effects include

- Parents not being able to provide their children with food, housing, stimulating toys, books, and experiences
- Parents themselves having poor emotional health because of the stresses that economic deprivation imposes on them, which may include being more depressed, irritable, or labile emotionally
- Parents being less consistent or more punitive in their punishment of their children
- Parents having less time to spend with their children and less energy to devote to the children's concerns when with them
- Parents having less ability to provide adequate child-care arrangements when they work or must be away from the children

Thus there are many different ways in which poverty affects children.

It is in the preschool years that children first construct a picture of their primary environment. Children in persistent poverty are apt to live in a world in which reality truly is harsh, depriving, and perhaps dangerous; that offers relatively few interesting objects that can be explored; in which caretakers are weary and prohibitory; and in which caretakers often have to defer to others in authority and seldom receive respect from those in authority. Such is the environment in which children living in poverty construct their identities. Since children construct their pictures of the world and of themselves through social participation (Nelson 1986), merely being aware (from television or other brief observations) that some people do not live in such difficult circumstances is unlikely to alter these pictures. The environment in which a child spends his or her early years is simply accepted by the child as "the way things are." The conditions under which such children live are not likely to facilitate the ability to transcontextualize, and they are thus left psychologically as well as economically captive to their environment.

Poor children are also more apt to live in environments where violence is more likely to occur; the parents must, therefore, teach their children that the world is violent in order to ensure their survival, yet in doing so they also may inhibit the expression of curiosity and exploration that contributes to the development of cognitive skills (Groves and Zuckerman 1997) and identity complexity. Fonagy and colleagues (1997) believe that crimes in adolescence "are often committed by individuals with inadequate mentalizing capacities, as part of their pathological attempt at adaptation to a social environment in which mentalization is essential" (164). Thus parents are in the double-binding position in which their attempts at ensuring the survival of their children may also contribute to the children becoming more likely to participate in violence in the community.

Considerable evidence is consistent with a perspective that the individual's construction of identity within a depriving environment plays a significant role in social control. There is, first, the simple fact that few real revolutions or major acts of protestation are undertaken by people in poverty-stricken environments, even when conditions are extremely harsh and inequitable. Wang (1999) notes that in power struggles people do not often look for the "chief enemy" but for the immediate one, and thus they more commonly take their frustrations out on one another rather than on those who are truly more advantaged. There are numerous studies (e.g., Duncan and Brooks-Gunn 1997) showing that children of school age whose families are economically disadvantaged have lower self-esteem and are less popular than are children from more advantaged families. Stevens (1996) has noted that pregnancy among impoverished adolescent girls appears to be motivated in part by an attempt to gain a respected adult role through becoming a mother and is, therefore, likely to be an effect of the girls' lack of alternative routes to adulthood.

In a fascinating study of engagement in narratives in preschool children, Wiley and co-workers (1998) found that mothers of preschool children in working-class families were more likely to engage their children in storytelling than were middle-class mothers, but the working-class mothers also provided the final word on the meaning of the story significantly more often; middle-class mothers were more likely to allow their children to retain their own points of view. Consistent with the findings of Wiley and colleagues, Schooler (1999), in a study of adult men, found that "the lower their social-stratification positions, the more men value conformity to external authority and the more they are convinced that conformity is all that their abilities and the nature of their circumstances allow" (239).

Children will, of course, have differences in the manner in which interactions with the environment are experienced. Those who have as caretakers more available and affectively attuned adults will have more opportunity to construct an identity that is complex and that can allow for transcontextualizing in other settings. Those whose environments are highly chaotic may find it difficult to achieve any stable event representations and therefore may have difficulty constructing an identity for themselves, thereby putting themselves at risk for serious mental illness. In addition, as Hernandez (1997) has pointed out, people are poverty stricken when their income is significantly lower than that of the community in which they live. There is a subjective element to the effects of poverty as well as one that can be measured by objective standards.

Perhaps because we all, consciously or subconsciously, are aware that our identity is in large part determined by an environment that we do not really control and that therefore includes the possibility of change in a negative direction, there is a common human tendency to want to keep some distance from those who are judged as indecent or degraded. In this regard, Benjamin (1988) observed:

The kind of social support that might spark our identification with the helplessness of the needy is bitterly resisted. This attitude generates a vicious cycle in which the unconscious revulsion against early states of dependency or helplessness is reinforced by the spectacle of those we left in the lurch. The visible consequences of our failure to provide socially organized nurturance—a safe holding environment—intensify our distance and disidentification from those who require support. Witness the refusal to recognize the increasing number of women and children below the poverty line. (203)

It follows that those whose material environments are stressful and deficient are also likely to find themselves abandoned by their fellow humans.

How, then, can psychotherapy—which, after all, is a form of intervention that works with individuals, families, and small groups rather than with public policy—contribute to lessening the domination of persons who are disadvantaged? If social control in current societies is exercised through subjectivities, then it is specifically psychotherapy's access to subjectivities that gives it the power either to consolidate domination or to contribute to freedom. It is important, however, to remember that treatment that imposes the therapist's own goals for the client cannot be freeing. Identity complexity and the ability to transcontextualize can be based only on the *client's* goals and experiences, and this complexity must begin with a reconciliation with the identity developed in the client's primary environment. In her discussion of identity in a racism-related stress, Harrell (2000) observed:

Worldview, cultural values, spirituality, and racial identity reflect deeply rooted internal aspects of the individual, which can provide (1) a connection with a larger racial, cultural, spiritual community; (2) a sense of meaning and understanding of one's life and world; and (3) a core foundation offering guidance and a framework for decision-making. Moreover, it has been suggested that a worldview consistent with one's racial/cultural group, strong racial identity, racism awareness, and a bicultural adaptation can furnish the racism-resistant armor needed to build positive well-being. Recent research has suggested that a strong attachment to one's identity group can buffer the negative effects of discrimination and increase self-esteem. By contrast, the internalization of racist beliefs and behavior, unacknowledged racial self-hatred, separation from one's racial/ethnic group, and belief in one's immunity to racism could exacerbate exposure to racism and increase the risk of maladaptive outcomes. (51)

Harrell's statement applies, of course, whether the identity group in question involves difference regarding race, class, sexual orientation, religion, or other similar factors.

Altman (1995) offers a number of examples of problematic issues occurring in the work of analytically oriented therapists in an inner-city public mental health clinic. These include the therapist's guilt over having more resources than the patient, his failure to understand things like the patient's frequently missing appointments, and so on. Such problems, of course, occur when neither therapist nor patient has ready access to event representations commonly formed from the environment of the other partner. It may well be impossible to eliminate such difficulties entirely, but having a theory that can encompass both the nature of the environment and specific information about the client's environment can certainly help.

CCORDING TO FREUD, sexuality plays an exemplary role in
that it is the underlying truth through which the analyst under-
stands the patient's ultimate unconscious meaning and the truth
through which all behaviors are to be interpreted. It was, for Freud,
however, an intrapsychic and biological function—natural, not social.
Yet, as Berger and Luckman (1966) and numerous anthropologists have
noted, all cultures have injunctions about what behaviors, with whom,
are permissible and what are forbidden. There is, however, considerable
variation in what is considered normal across cultures. The manner in
which sexuality is expressed is dictated by culture and structured by
society. As Seidman (1998) has indicated, "The system of sexuality is
built into the fabric of our institutions (e.g., state, law, medical clinics,
hospitals and family), cultural apparatus (e.g., mass media, advertising,
and educational system, church), and into the very texture of everyday
life (e.g., customs, norms, language, and lifestyle ideals)" (241). Sexuality, like other aspects of culture, is therefore both internal and
environmental.

Sexuality plays a crucial role in the theories of both Freud and Foucault, but their stances regarding it are almost diametrically opposed.
For Freud, primitive sexual impulses were alien to the ego and were
therefore rendered unconscious through powerful forces of repression.
Foucault (1990), however, argued that the repression of sexuality is a
myth:

> Rather than the uniform concern to hide sex, rather than a general
> prudishness of language, what distinguishes these last three cen-
> turies is the variety, the wide dispersion of devices that were
> invented for speaking about it, for having it be spoken about, for
> inducing it to speak of itself, for listening, recording, transcribing,
> and redistributing what is said about it: around sex, a whole net-

work of varying, specific, and coercive transpositions into discourse. . . .

What is peculiar to modern societies, in fact, is not that they con-
signed sex to a shadow existence, but that they dedicated themselves to speaking of it *ad infinitum*, while exploiting it, as *the*
secret [italics in original]. (34–35)

For Foucault, the ever-present discourse about sexuality was one of
the prominent means through which subjectivities of dominance are
constructed.

Foucault (1995; Parton 1999) saw *discipline* as the manner in which
social control is enforced in current Western societies. Discipline
involves three processes, inseparable in their functioning, but important
to understand together in order to grasp the effectiveness of the control
exercised. Although Foucault's ideas about discipline were originally
formulated in a study of penal institutions, he considered them to be
equally characteristic of psychotherapy:

1. *Hierarchical surveillance* is the continual oversight of the body
of the subject by others with more power. For the individual, this
monitoring is not only continual, but also inescapable. There is
nothing that can be hidden from this inspection. In classical conceptions of psychoanalysis, of course, the surveillance extends itself
to thoughts and impulses of which the patient is not even aware.
The patient, though, is not to know anything about the analyst's
life, since this knowledge would disrupt the "blank screen" and
thereby the therapy. Should the patient comment on some observation about the analyst, this was to be interpreted in terms of the
patient's inner life. The surveillance was nonreciprocal.

2. *Normalizing judgment* is the evaluation and classification of
the behavior, including thinking, of the subject. This judgment is
made according to a scale that runs from good to bad, but the
determinants involved are not always apparent to the subject and
may even seem quite arbitrary. In psychotherapy, psychiatric diag-
noses are presumed to be scientific; the *DSM*, however, has under-
gone numerous revisions and qualifications in an attempt to make
it more exact, and even with the five axes it is still easy for different
clinicians to rate the same client and the same clinical material
differently.

3. *The examination* combines the processes of surveillance and normalization, making it possible for the examiner to classify the subject in terms that have significant consequences for the individual's status, including, but not limited to, the possibility of removal from society into a hospital or penal institution. Thus the examination not only can result in an assault to the patient's narcissism, but can have real consequences in decisions affecting the individual's life—the custody of a child, for example. The psychotherapist is, however, not the only societally endorsed examiner. Courts and other institutions also act in this manner, and the psychotherapist may not always agree with the final judgment. The examination is pervasive in society, ensuring that even if no actual judgment is made, the subject will be sufficiently intimidated by the possibility of such judgment as to be rendered docile and conforming in the face of the existing power structures. Psychotherapists both exercise power within the social structure and are themselves subject to it. Like all citizens, psychotherapists are enveloped within the structures of power.

Power relations in sexual matters are exercised through *scientia sexualis*—that is, dealing with sexuality as a science in which behaviors can be studied, classified, and manipulated. According to Foucault (1990; O'Brien 1999), the science of sexuality is exercised in at least four arenas:

1. Women's bodies are *hysterized* so that the ultimate control of their sexual and reproductive functions is carried out by others, ordinarily men.
2. Procreation is *socialized* so that there is control over who is to reproduce and under what conditions they may legitimately do so.
3. Through *pedagogization* of children's sexuality, the young are taught acceptable means of sexual expression and chastened if they do not behave in accord with societal expectations.
4. Through the *psychiatrization* of the perversions, guilt over means of sexual expression—even if it be promoted by the culture—can be evoked and manipulated for conservative political ends.

Discourse in each of these areas operates in a manner that both makes the underlying power operations invisible and convinces those who are subject to those operations that the status quo either is in their own best interest or is simply a part of a natural process.

There are numerous examples of the ways in which psychoanalytic theory can be understood to have promoted domination of the kind Foucault (1990) charged. For example, recent feminist theory has called attention to problems in classical theory, such as assuming that "anatomy is destiny," that motherhood is natural, that problems in adulthood arise from poor mothering, and that the hormone cycles in women make them less suitable for jobs that require rational judgments. Yet recently, both Benjamin (1988, 1998) and Butler (1990) have noted that even some recent feminist analytic theorists have contributed to the continuation of gender inequality through an acceptance of the binary, oppositional status of male–female. This, they declare, simply perpetuates the definition of women in terms of that which is not male.

Foucault (1990) pointed out that while homosexual behavior has existed throughout the history of the world, it was not until the eighteenth century that there was a "homosexual person"; thereafter, since same-sex attractions were presumed to be perverse, this meant that the whole individual was perverse—not merely in sexual behavior, but in all aspects of functioning. Thus psychoanalytic constructions of sexuality have also contributed to the domination of gay men and lesbian women. In this area as well, however, some who have wished to further the gay-liberation movement have become caught up in a discussion about whether homosexuality is fundamentally determined by genetic characteristics or by individual choice, when actually the issue ought to be that same-sex behaviors are acceptable regardless of any underlying causal factors.

That the constructs of psychoanalytic theory in regard to sexuality can and have contributed to the domination of those the therapy was intended to cure appears to be incontrovertible. Theories of psychotherapy are invariably a part of the cultures in which they arise and are constantly interacting with other aspects of that culture. Understanding whether, and how, psychotherapy can contribute to resistance in relation to the sphere of sexuality requires additional exploration of the meaning of sexual experience in human life.

THE PSYCHOLOGICAL FUNCTION OF SEXUALITY

IN CONTRAST TO FREUD, who thought that sexuality was the essence of the personality, Foucault (1990) did not regard sexuality per se as having any special meaning or place in human life. Yet sexuality does have a very central place in all human cultures, which suggests the possibility that sexuality indeed plays a special role, beyond that of reproduction, in human life. In an interesting but not widely cited book, Heinz Lichtenstein (1977) raised the interesting question, "What is the psychological function of non-procreative sexuality?" His answer: "I suggest that we attribute to sexuality an 'affirmative function' and that we define this term as the principle that sexuality constitutes the primary, most archaic, and nonverbal mode through which the conviction of one's existence is affirmed as an incontrovertible truth. I would like to emphasize the terms 'primary and most archaic,' because it is obvious that in the course of development other modes become available" (275). The erogenous zones do produce sensations of a different and more intense nature than other parts of the body and therefore may be especially equipped to serve in the primary manner that Lichtenstein proposed. However, as Klein (1976) noted, sensuality is highly plastic and can be aroused by a variety of stimuli. Thus although the function may be a common element across cultures, the exact nature of the sexual behavior in which the person engages is likely to be individually and culturally determined.

Although Lichtenstein's proposal regarding the affirmative function of orgasm was housed within ego psychology and Benjamin's concept of recognition is housed in a contemporary relational viewpoint, the two conceptions appear to complement each other. Benjamin (1988) said: "In my view, the simultaneous desire for loss of self and for wholeness (or oneness) with the other, often described as the ultimate point of erotic union, is really a form of desire for recognition. In getting pleasure *with* the other and taking pleasure *in* the other, we engage in mutual recognition [italics in original]" (126). Both conceptions see orgasm as an experience in which there can be a potentially powerful affirmation of self.

Lichtenstein's (1977) theory has considerable explanatory power. For example,

- Sexual behavior is not "the same as shaking hands," and under ordinary conditions the choice of partner is important because the intimacy involved in confirming one's fundamental sense of existence is not something to be shared with just anyone.
- Some forms of extreme stress tend to lead to increased sexual behavior, which may serve to assure the person that his own psychological continuity is intact.

• It is not uncommon for someone who has experienced a major loss, such as the death of a spouse, to find herself becoming more involved with others sexually than ever before. Often this may be distressing for the individual, who may wonder if this is a statement that she did not care for the lost partner as much as she thought, although the behavior may mean only that there is now a need for a sense that "life goes on."
• People of either sex who flaunt their sexuality in exhibitionistic ways are often not accomplished lovers, but people whose self-esteem is weak and who need to rely on sexuality for confirmation of their identity more than do others.
• People who are threatened by psychological fragmentation may engage in sexual behavior in order to attain a sense of being more centered.

A case in point is that of Mr. Norman:

Mr. Norman, a forty-seven-year-old married man with two grown children, was seen for treatment in conjunction with his request for assistance with a problem with erectile dysfunction. Diagnosis ultimately indicated that the primary cause was medical, with a basis in some vascular problems. However, Mr. Norman also complained of chronic depression, marital problems, and irritability with others. He had been married for twenty-six years and at first experienced this relationship, including its sexual aspects, as a good one, but it began deteriorating shortly after the birth of his second child. At that time, Mr. Norman, usually regularly employed in a skilled blue-collar job, had been temporarily laid off. The resulting economic necessity led his wife to obtain a job, at which she continued even after Mr. Norman was able to return to work. Mr. Norman dated his erectile problems to the period of unemployment, but noted that it had become worse over the years.

Since the sexual-dysfunction clinic ordinarily preferred to work with both partners in a sexual relationship, Mr. Norman was requested to involve his wife in the treatment. However, Mr. Norman refused to do so, and only after establishing a comfortable relationship with a psychotherapist was he able to explain the reason for his reluctance. When his wife first began working, Mr. Norman began to experience sexual intercourse with his wife as disquieting in some way and would some-times leave the house after having intercourse with her, going to a local bar. There he met a male prostitute, and sometimes he would have a second sexual encounter, which he experienced as pleasurable. Over time, he stopped having intercourse with his wife but continued to seek out the services of a male prostitute. Yet in time, even the experience with a prostitute became unpleasant. Thus he began to rely solely on masturbation, using a pair of his wife's panties as a sexual stimulant. He believed that his wife did not care about the loss of sexual relations in the marriage, and he did not want to return to having intercourse with her. He did, however, want his masturbatory experiences to be more satisfying than they had become.

Mr. Norman, an illegitimate child, had been raised by an aunt who had fundamentalist religious convictions. He had always felt rather like a male Cinderella, although minus the fairy godmother, in com-parison with his cousins—the legitimate children of his aunt and uncle. Later in life, he had sought out both of his natural parents but found that neither had much interest in him. Mr. Norman left home as soon as he thought he could support himself and married relatively young, partly as a means of securing a comfortable environment in which his basic daily needs could be met. He had been a reliable employee and a good provider for his family, but had assumed a rather passive role in all his relationships, seemingly having assumed that he would always remain on the periphery of life's important activities. Mr. Norman's self-confidence and sense of ability to influence his environment were not well developed, a condition that appears to have been chronic.*

Lichtenstein (1977) pointed out that Freud (1923) and many others had characterized the psychological experience of orgasm as "a little death" that is pleasurable because after a very short time the sense of being alive and reinvigorated follows. Yet for some people, allowing this little death to occur is frightening because the sense of continuity—of "going on being," to use Winnicott's (1958) term—is too fragile and the person cannot risk the possibility of its not returning following the orgasm. This appeared to be the case with Mr. Norman. The fear of los-

---

*This case was previously presented and discussed in C. Saari, *Clinical social work treat-ment: How does it work?* (New York: Gardner Press, 1986).

ing a sense of identity can be increased if the sexual activity includes a partner, since the orgasm can seem like a temporary merger with that other person. Here Winnicott's (1965b) idea that human beings can lose their identity if either fused with another person or isolated from others helps to understand why orgasm for someone like Mr. Norman would be less threatening if it occurred only when he was alone. The ability to trust that an invigorated self will return after the brief but intense merger with an intimate other seems to be a developmental achievement that occurs in late adolescence and is the reason to suggest to adolescents that, if possible, they postpone intercourse until they have achieved some degree of psychological stability. The fear of loss of identity may well be the underlying reason for psychological impotence in men and frigidity in women.

"THE MALIGNANT NO"

WITHIN HEALTHY SEXUAL intimacy, the person becomes the instrument for the fulfillment of the other person's needs, but within sexual interactions there is also the possibility of the other person's negating rather than affirming one's identity. Lichtenstein (1977) used the term "the malignant NO" to refer to the particularly pernicious combination of a negative evaluation of the individual and a prohibition of conditions that make possible positive identity maintenance. He believed that, just as human beings need and seek out experiences that affirm their fundamental sense of identity, so do they fear that the identity will be negated rather than affirmed. While the malignant NO can operate in relation to any area of human functioning, rape is the ultimate example because it consists essentially of one person's confirmation of his or her identity while totally negating that of the other. Rape victims, it should be recalled, ordinarily describe what the rape caused as "I no longer know who I am." A similar example of the malignant NO is that of child sexual abuse.

The malignant NO, however, also occurs in nonsexual ways in which dominating subjectivities are created within certain groups considered to be deviant. In such instances, members of the group in question are labeled negatively and then blamed for having that negative characteristic. An example is that of considering African Americans to be lazy or fundamentally dependent while denying them access to quality education and the employment opportunities available to others. In the area of sexuality, the malignant NO can be seen in the invisibility often experienced by lesbians. That which is considered deviant and perverse is not to be allowed a place in public discourse.

The access to dialogues through which to arrive at shared meaning with others and the ability to participate in and feel part of the surrounding human community is often not readily available to lesbians and gay men. The denial of the ability to participate in public rituals such as marriage and, sometimes, even the funeral of a life partner limits the opportunity to create a sense of a life that is meaningful in terms of the surrounding society. When this occurs, the individual is likely to have a constricted range of possible meanings for life. It limits the recognition of options for behavior and for an envisioned future. In other words, the malignant NO conditions that are imposed on lesbians and gay men can result in a less well-developed and complex identity than might otherwise have been possible. Further, this societal condition is likely to affect all people with same-sex attractions, although, of course, those who have had more favorable conditions for development in their early environment will be able to manage the stresses of an openly homosexual life more easily, and those whose development has been more problematic will likely have more difficulty.

Narrative, the form in which adult identity is ordinarily captured and expressed (Bruner 1990; Gergen 1994; Saari 1991; Schafer 1992), plays a particularly important role in the treatment of same-sex couples because, amid the stresses of living in a homophobic society, the story of the relationship is critical to the survival of a loving relationship. Perhaps the most important thing that holds couples together, whether they are hetero- or homosexual, is the sharing of experiences and the sharing of a sense of "we-ness." For heterosexual couples, there are many social settings in which the partners are routinely expected to talk about their story. While they include ritual celebrations, such as weddings and anniversary parties, there are also less formal occasions in which two or more couples participate. Such events provide a couple with practice in constructing and refining their story as well as affirmation of the significance of the relationship. Except in totally gay circles, however, same-sex partners are rarely called on to do this because there is an unconscious assumption on the part of heterosexual individuals that the stories of gay couples might involve elements that are shameful. The lack of opportunities for gay couples to celebrate their relationship through telling their story is a subtle but very real example of the increased stress with which same-sex couples must cope. Helping a gay couple construct or relate a story of their relationship in treatment (as in the following case history) is, therefore, very significant.

Martha, then aged forty-five, and Estella, then twenty-eight, had met at a conference of the political party in which both were active volunteers. At the time, Martha was married, had two adolescent children, and was living in an upper-class suburban area in the Midwest. Estella was single and living in Puerto Rico, where she had grown up; she did not have a college degree, but was employed by a nonprofit volunteer agency. When they met, both experienced a powerful attraction: they confessed this to each other, but no sexual activity occurred. They corresponded for a short time, and then Estella quit her job and moved to the city near where Martha lived, determined to follow her impulses regarding the only romance she had ever experienced. For a time, Martha, although fond of Estella, resisted her enticing overtures and felt ashamed of her attraction to a woman. Estella, however, was persistent, and her attempts at seduction were ultimately successful. Martha took a part-time job and then gave Estella enough money to live comfortably and to obtain a college degree. Estella was presented to Martha's family and friends as someone she liked very much and had agreed to assist. Estella, for her part, never told her family about the real nature of the relationship because she saw homosexuality as totally unacceptable in Puerto Rico; this was not difficult because her family had little money, and no one came to visit her.

Martha was insistent that her children had to be her first priority and that she could not leave her marriage until they were in college. She wondered what others thought of her relationship with Estella, but no one seemed to suspect its nature and she continued to be involved in a number of social groups within her community, sometimes taking Estella with her. While Estella found it difficult to deal with this relationship while pretending that she and Martha were simply friends, she thought that she would be willing to endure anything in order to preserve her relationship with Martha. Eight years after Estella's move, Martha's children were in college. By then, Estella had completed her college degree and had obtained an entry-level position in her chosen field. Martha then obtained a "friendly divorce" from her husband and even took Estella with her when she attended his second wedding.

Martha and Estella obtained an apartment together and initially reveled in their new freedom. Martha, however, was struggling with her new life, fearing that acquaintances and friends from her previous life would learn about Estella and that her children would be disgraced. Their relationship, which both had experienced as sustaining in the early years, now became stressful, with Estella fearing that she would lose Martha after all the years she had waited for her. Only two or three friends knew of their love for each other. Then Martha's son, having completed college, became engaged and asked his mother how he should describe Estella to his future in-laws. Martha thought that he had either guessed or been told of his father's suspicions. Begging him not to tell anyone else, Martha confessed the truth. Martha then talked with one of the few friends who had been in her confidence and received the name of an openly lesbian therapist who could see them as a couple.

At Martha and Estella's initial presentation for couples therapy, they appeared to be an unlikely couple—very different from each other. Martha gave the impression of a very attractive and feminine well-to-do suburban matron with a northern European background. Estella, who had a darker complexion, hair, and eyes and who indicated that she could talk about emotions more easily in her native Spanish, wore slacks, had short hair, and had the slightly masculine air that in the lesbian community is referred to as "soft butch." Yet both said they were committed to their relationship and wanted to learn more about "how to be comfortable as lesbians." Although their relationship had already lasted for more than nine years, neither knew anything about the gay and lesbian media or about how to meet other lesbians; they were delighted with information about how to find the local newspaper and the women's bookstore.

Martha felt at a loss as to how to talk with people about her relationship with Estella, but she wanted to reassure Estella that she was committed to it. Many people already knew Estella, but they had assumed that the relationship was nonsexual. Martha thought that explaining to others that there really was a sexual relationship would be demeaning to her, so she did not want to tell her acquaintances. Martha feared that people would think the relationship was pathological because she was nearly old enough to be Estella's mother. She insisted that she had never felt maternal toward Estella, commenting, "Can't you see how gorgeous she is?" Martha, nevertheless, was insistent that she was not a lesbian, but was bisexual. Estella seemed far less concerned about how others might view them, but noted that she did not have the same problems as Martha, since she did not have family or long-term friends in the area. Estella declared herself as wanting to support Martha and not to force her to be more open than she wanted.

Nevertheless, most of the discussions in the weekly therapy sessions centered around how they could best present themselves to others. As they were still establishing themselves in living together, there were repeated arenas in which the question was raised of who should know what. Invariably, Martha would wish to avoid any mention of what she saw as her private behavior, and, just as invariably, Estella would feel rejected by what she experienced as Martha's wish to deny the relationship. It was necessary, over and over again, to help them make a distinction between commitment to their relationship and presenting that relationship to others—they had to make decisions about how to handle both areas. In part, Martha and Estella expressed some relief just knowing that their issues were common problems faced by most lesbians.

It is likely, however, that what was most useful to Martha and Estella was reviewing and narrating the history of their relationship. Their strengths were evident as they talked, and the discussions helped them to see this. Both were asked how they had experienced critical moments in time, which helped remind them of how important they were to each other. Estella could reexperience Martha's commitment to her throughout the years together, and Martha could recognize that some of what she had presented as concern about her children was really based in her fears of rejection from others and in the stress of her lifestyle transition. Their mutual commitment to making a success of their life together could thus be supported.

Although Martha had become comfortable in talking about her relationship with Estella with her son, she was far more frightened of talking with her daughter. She knew that Estella was right that the daughter would eventually learn of it from her brother and that Martha needed to initiate a discussion so that the daughter would hear it from her. With Estella's support, Martha did tell her daughter, who abruptly left, saying that she wanted no further contact with Estella and maybe not with her mother. Although Martha was somewhat despondent over this rupture, she came to recognize that the daughter would come around in time and that at this point in her life her own needs and her relationship with Estella had to assume center stage. Estella was reassured that she really did come first in Martha's life. This major hurdle over, Martha and Estella were able to work out ways of making apparent to others the nature of their relationship in a way that Martha could tolerate; for example, they bought ornate matching wedding bands that would make a statement about their relationship without their having to address it directly. At the time of the termination of therapy, both women felt confident that they could work together on ways to solve the problems involved in making themselves comfortably visible in a homophobic society.*

SHAME

MARTHA'S MAJOR DILEMMA, common for many homosexuals, was that she could choose to resist the culture's proscription of discourse about homosexuality and thereby to behave in a way that was affirming her own and Estella's identities as well as their life together. If she did this, however, she also placed herself in a position in which the bedrock of her own identity, that of her sexuality, would be exposed to the possibility of negation. This is, therefore, clearly a decision that only Martha could make. Should a decision be imposed on her—for example, from a belief that all homosexuals should be open about their sexuality—the therapy would simply have shifted the site of Martha's domination. It would have exposed her to more negation and would certainly not have liberated her.

Exposure to the negation of one's fundamental sense of existence brings on an acute sense of shame. Nathanson (1992) has pointed out that "shame hovers everywhere in the bed of lust" (300). He noted that the degree of shame that we may experience when a sexual relationship goes sour is correlated with the degree to which we believed we would

---

*A discussion of this case is also in C. Saari, "Counteracting the effects of invisibility in work with lesbian clients," *Journal of Clinical Psychology: In Session* 57 (2001): 645–654.

find contentment within that relationship. Nathanson also makes a distinction between shame and guilt. Guilt occurs when we believe we have acted in some way that is either harmful or socially prohibited, whereas shame involves the very quality of our person or self; whereas an act can be forgotten or forgiven, the quality of our selves, our identity, presumably persists. Shame, therefore, is the more powerful of the two emotional states.

As was illustrated in the work with Martha and Estella, some discussions around sexuality in psychotherapy can be liberating; indeed, because of the special importance of sexuality in human functioning and in the operation of potentially dominating cultural discourses, discussions in psychotherapy about sexual matters can have powerfully positive effects. However, because sexuality opens the person to *both affirmation and negation* of the fundamental sense of self, a therapist ought to tread these waters with the utmost of caution. A psychotherapist must first be sure that the client is feeling sufficiently secure in the treatment relationship, that there is sufficient comfort with intimacy to allow for sharing sexual material. Ordinarily, it is better to wait for the client to introduce sexual topics. Yet even when the client has raised such issues, the therapist must be sure that whatever he or she says will be heard as an affirmation rather than as a negation and that the client does not feel too exposed or too vulnerable.

Winnicott (1965b), who used the word *impingement* to describe something that interrupts the infant's ability to achieve an integrated self, believed that analytic interpretations can be impingements. Freud may have been right that sexuality plays a special function in human life—although drive theory may not have been the best way to understand that special function. Surely, many analytic interpretations that were centered around sexuality as Freud directed must have been experienced as impingements, as a contemporary reading of the Dora case illustrates. Indeed, such interpretations may well threaten the individual's fundamental sense of an enduring and cohesive identity—Winnicott's "going on being." Nathanson (1992:285) commented that the ultimate development of sexuality is for it to become play—an idea with which Winnicott (1971a) would surely agree.

PART 3 / IMPLICATIONS FOR PRACTICE

THE CONTENT OF A psychoanalytic session has always dealt with the patient's experience, but in orthodox analysis it was believed that the patient was cured through the revelation of his or her unconscious mind, which could be unearthed almost as in an archaeological dig. Thus the patient's experience was understood and interpreted according to Freud's theory of the intrapsychic world. Increasingly, however, psychoanalytic theory is abandoning this perspective. Instead, as Stern (1997) has indicated, psychoanalysis is being understood as a forum in which curiosity and the acceptance of uncertainty are tolerated and thereby allow for the emergence of ideas that have never been thought before. In this newer understanding, the patient is thought to be helped to "create personal meaning" (78). Yet what is that meaning to be like? What is it to be based on? Will any meaning do? To date, relatively little attention has been paid to the nature of content in a constructivist approach, and it is in considering this problem that Rubin (1997) noted the "problem for the practitioner is that 'anything goes' is not acceptable, but new frameworks are still in the process of developing" (6).

Currently developing theories emphasize that the patient's experience is interpreted through a process of co-construction of its meaning within the interaction of patient and analyst. Many postmodern therapists agree that therapist–client interactions result in a shared vision of reality that has been constructed through dialogue (Aron 1996; Benjamin 1999; Mitchell 1998; Stern 1997). Ogden (1994) says that there are three subjectivities involved in treatment: the analyst's, the patient's, and the "analytic third," which the two participants create mutually. Along these lines, Saari (1986) indicated that

client growth . . . generally requires more than simply a working alliance. It requires a context within which to exercise and practice the functioning of the self system. It requires, in fact, a culture within the treatment situation itself. Human relationships do not and cannot operate without a social environment and a social meaning system. The therapeutic relationship is no exception. The worker and the client, therefore, together utilize their relationship to create between them a culture within which to foster the client's growth. It is because of and within this cultural system that the worker and the client can communicate with each other. It is also within this culture that the client and the worker will examine and define the meaning of their relationship and of the world of reality. (209)

Saari used the word *concordance* to describe this therapeutic culture, and has since seen such concordances as central to the curative effect of psychotherapy. The reality-processing skills that were practiced in the treatment are then used by the client in cultures and relationships outside the treatment setting.

Theory in which the construction of a shared vision of reality—a concordance—plays a significant role cannot avoid taking some perspective on the environment, however. It is, as Moore (1999) indicated, the patient's problems in interacting with his or her everyday world that have led this person to seek treatment in the first place. Cavell (1993) has claimed that theories of treatment *must* take the external world into account: "On the view I have been championing, the world itself is what we have been in touch with all along. It is neither behind (or beyond) talk, nor constituted by it" (116). Stern (1997) believes that "the human being and the world around him are a unity, that person and world both participate in the creation of experience" (168). At another point, Stern describes the nature of self–environment interactions:

I am proposing that the outer world plays an independent role in establishing which parts of the inner one—which selves—are relevant at any particular moment. The influence cuts both ways, in other words. The outer world, by setting the limits on what the field can be, helps to determine what parts of the inner world are relevant. The inner world influences what parts of the outer world we select and try to encounter, and what parts of those selected aspects of the outer world we try to bring into active relatedness with us. The relationship of the inner and outer worlds is dialectical, with each the primary ingredient in the recipe for the other. (155–156)

The outer worlds of both therapist and client are dynamic entities and are present in the clinical interactions. They also contribute to the concordance that is created in the treatment.

The concept of a shared reality or a concordance helps to solve some other conceptual problems. For example, psychoanalytic theory, beginning with Freud, has supposed that the patient is experiencing an intrapsychic conflict and that this is a major part of the motivation for treatment. In conceptualizing relational theory, Mitchell (1998) and other theorists aligned with this perspective have wanted to retain the centrality of conflict, thereby using "relational-conflict theory" to characterize their perspective. For some psychotherapy clients, however, conflict is not a significant part of their experience at all. Instead, they experience a profound emptiness that can be quite debilitating. To acknowledge this is not to deny Aron's (1996) point that "*conflict is inherent in relatedness*" (160), but to indicate that not all clients have developed the ability to *experience* that conflict. Ordinarily, these clients have been understood, not through conflict theory but rather through positing a deficit theory.

Mitchell (1988), however, has argued eloquently against a deficit theory, saying that such theory involves infantilizing the patient by the assumption that this person is like a baby whom the psychotherapist must "raise" through parenting that is better than that received in childhood. The danger of infantilizing the client is certainly present in a theory that takes Freud's concept of regression in a literal sense. Yet while the ability to create meaning and a rich internal life does begin in childhood, the skills involved with this are practiced throughout life and can be influenced for good or ill at any time in the life cycle. Psychotherapy, as conceptualized here, does not reverse the cause of a client's problems, does not even necessarily address or know the cause(s) of the problem; rather, it helps the client deal with the negative effects on meaning-making functioning that have occurred, regardless of the cause. Thus psychotherapy works by helping the client learn and practice meaning-making skill rather than by reversing the reasons why the skill was not developed at an earlier time in life. Such a theoretical position need not deny the importance of intrapsychic conflict, which can indeed be a problem for many clients, but it also can work well with clients for whom conflict is not a central part of their daily experience.

Is it necessary to assume that the conclusions reached in the concordance are objectively true, that they are a correct deciphering of what is in the client's mind? Here both Mitchell (1998:16) and Stern (1997:39) argue, correctly I think, that there is no such location as a "mind," but that the mind is composed of complex sets of processes through which the person arrives at particular conclusions about the self and the world that are germane to the moment and the situation at hand. Both authors indicate that the conclusions in what I am calling the concordance must fit well with the patient's sense of self in both the past and the present, but that these conclusions should never be seen as final or definitive.

CHANGING VIEWS OF THE UNCONSCIOUS

UNDERSTANDING THE currently changing views of the unconscious helps to clarify the nature of the therapeutic culture and its construction. Freud's unconscious was, of course, the result of repression—the human inability to tolerate anxiety. In infancy, the organism had to use a barrier in order to avoid becoming totally overwhelmed by the anxiety caused by too much stimulation that could not yet be processed, and this barrier led to amnesia. Today, however, this amnesia is thought to be explained best through the assumption that the brain of the infant operates on the physiological process of implicit memory rather than by repression, anxiety, or defense (Amini et al. 1996). Further maturation of the brain (involving interactions between the person and the environment) is necessary before the explicit-memory system to which the individual has conscious access can become operative. Implicit memory, however, continues to function throughout life. Stolorow and Atwood (1992) have called attention to something similar in "the *prereflective unconscious*—the organizing principles that unconsciously shape and thematize the person's experiences" (33).

In recent years, however, several different types of unconscious have been described in the literature. Stolorow and Atwood (1992) identify two other types: "the *dynamic unconscious*—experiences that were denied articulation because they were perceived to threaten needed ties to others; and . . . the *unvalidated unconscious*—experiences that could not be articulated because they never evoked the requisite validating responsiveness from human others" (33). Note that Stolorow and Atwood's conception of the dynamic unconscious is intersubjective. For them, this unconscious content is not too threatening because of its primitive drive aspects, but because of its threat to a needed interpersonal tie. Further, their unvalidated unconscious also is relational since in this regard it is the failure of the responsiveness of the human environment that is the factor in determining that which makes the experience unrecognizable. Stern (1985) has a concept similar to the unvalidated unconscious. He claims that inner experience that is not affectively attuned cannot be shared with others and, presumably, not with the self. Humans are social beings who need interactions with one another in order to be able to create meaning.

Stern (1997), rather than using the term *unconscious,* employs *unformulated experience*; in his view, the person simply may not notice that which he or she does not wish to know, and thus some potential content may remain unformulated because of selective perception. Selective perception may be rooted in two different elements, however. The significance of an aspect present in the environment may not have occurred to the individual, or there may be a defensive process that has made experiencing this aspect undesirable. Stern then notes:

> The basic defensive process must be the *prevention of interpretation* in reflective awareness, not the *exclusion from awareness* of elements that are already fully formed. If reflective experience is created by interpretation, such experience is avoided by not interpreting, or by not-spelling-out. And not interpreting, or not-spelling-out, are essentially ways to define dissociation. Defensively motivated unformulated experience, then, or what I have referred to as "familiar chaos," is the way the dynamic unconscious looks in a constructivist, dissociation-based model. Familiar chaos is to dissociation what repressed content is to repression. (87)

My preferred way to understand the unconscious is to look at it through the lens of Nelson's (1985) tripartite theory of meaning. Nelson's ideas can be used to create five useful categories.

First there is the *unexperienced*, or that which is potential experience—experience that the person has not encountered. This includes, of course, not only ways of thinking but also environmental elements to which the person has not been exposed. Clearly, verbal interpretation in treatment about something the client has never experienced will not be effective. It will be recalled that Nelson says that human beings learn through social participation; thus for the client to be able to connect experience to any personal meaning system, the unexperienced first must be encountered. This encounter may occur either in the treatment sessions or in the world beyond the treatment. For example, there are clients, particularly abused children, who literally have no experience of a truly caretaking adult. Such a client needs exposure to a wider circle of adults, but since the child has also constructed an identity as that of someone who evokes punishment from caretakers, it may be difficult for this child to see the adult's caring behavior as genuine.

The *unconstructed* exists when the person has participated in an environment and has event representations of what occurs in this environment, but the particular aspect of the environment in question has not been noted for its significance to the representation of the self and the world. Such a person may be able to call to mind the presence of this particular aspect if prompted or challenged to do so. When requested in therapy to describe his father in detail and asked what his father did with his time, John might realize that he had never thought about this before and did not know how his father chose to use free time. Then John might remember that his father spent a lot of time alone on the sunporch, looking at the view of the hills across the valley. This can eventuate in a realization that perhaps the father was depressed.

The *uninterpreted* exists when the person has the experience and may be able to call on nonverbal senses of its meaning, but the experience remains vague, ill-defined, because the person has not put this experience into a verbal form in which it can be reflected on. Freud (1915) thought that what made the difference between that which was conscious and that which was unconscious was that the conscious material could be connected with words in the language. On this basis, Basch (1983) referred to the uninterpreted as repression. Alice, a professional flutist, always found herself uncomfortable when she played in front of her mother, but she had never been able to put this discomfort into words—that she feared her mother's criticism.

There is the *unintegrated*, which in some senses is the reverse of the uninterpreted. The person has the language for some experience, but cannot connect those words with a meaningful inner experience. Nelson's (1985) theory would indicate that this person has the semantic level of meaning but not the conceptual level. The words used have connections to other words, but not to experience. Basch (1983) referred to the unintegrated as dissociation. The therapist must be alert to the fact that simply using words in treatment will not be sufficient to help the client. The experience that fits with the words must also be present. Richard's father always said that he cared about him, and Richard had always thought this was true; yet Richard could not experience loving feelings toward his own son, and later he realized that he could not recall his father having done much that demonstrated his caring.

Finally, there is the *cultural* unconscious, which includes the infinite number of ways in which experience or life can be understood but that have as yet to be constructed within the culture.

The orthodox understanding of the psychoanalytic process was that present symptoms were used to uncover unconscious meanings that would reveal the causes of the difficulties, and thereby to use an understanding of the past to undo the problems. Current constructivist understandings of treatment instead say that the past is reinterpreted in order to make the present more meaningful. Erikson (1975) said it this way: "I could not look at my patients' troubles any more in (what I later came to call) 'originological' terms—that is, on the basis of where, when, and how 'it all started.' The question was also what world image they were sharing, where they were going from where they were, and who was going with them"(44).

NARRATIVE FORM

THE ASSUMPTION THAT narrative form is intrinsic to human thought (Bruner 1986, 1990; Polkinghorne 1988) has become so well accepted in the mental health professions that the literature is now replete with it (Holma and Aaltonen 1995; Saari 1991; Schafer 1980, 1983, 1992; Susko 1994). The concordance, and personal experience in general, is now thought to be constructed in narrative form, a format that does have major advantages for psychotherapeutic endeavors. Susko (1994) provides a succinct list of aspects of narrative, which

- Can convey the thickness and richness of life events
- Can convey complex notions of the self (and multiple selves)
- Can allow for the recognition that life events and patterns are dynamic forces acting in the present
- Have the "fit of truth," but not proof
- Can allow people to emancipate themselves from the larger dominant cultural story
- Allow a true dialogue with another person through entering that person's story while retaining one's own identity

- Can allow for the integration of differing aspects of self and/or experience
- Can awaken love through the sharing of stories
- Can dignify one's communication to the larger society, exposing realities that are not usually allowed expression

Since narratives are interpretive constructions rather than inscribed truth, every story can be told in a number of ways, and many different stories can be told about any one event or experience.

Loewald (1960) believed that psychoanalysis allows for an organization and experiencing of self at many different levels, with varying degrees of integration, differentiation, and articulation. Healthy functioning, he thought, requires an orchestrated functioning that includes differing degrees of rationality or irrationality, depending on the situation at hand. Narrative form outlines plot, character, and setting in an integrated manner and can interweave a variety of themes or subplots in order to achieve the kind of orchestrated functioning that Loewald had in mind. Yet narrative is not just an organizer. Autobiographical narrative is also a natural form for the kind of reflexive thought that is characteristic of therapy. In autobiographical narrative, the teller is converted into two different selves: the protagonist, who is the center of the story, and the narrator, who reflects on the actions of the protagonist. Both selves have connections to the external world—the narrator to the world of the listeners, and the protagonist to the settings and characters of the story.

Unlike chronologies, narrative form includes the events and experiences that are germane to the explanation of the particular point the teller is attempting to make. Therefore, a coherent narrative selects the events relevant to the elucidation of the meaning the teller wishes to convey. In that sense, then, narratives highlight that which is important and omit that which is not, in this way making clear the client's perspective on the world that he or she inhabits. Yet a story can be effective only if its elements are convincing to the hearer. The culture within which the teller and the hearer function sets some limits on the believability of the story. This is true at the level of the general culture (a delusion, for example, can be understood to be a cherished belief that is not sanctioned by the sociocultural surround); it is, however, also true at the level of the concordance, which must include events and perspectives that seem genuine to both therapist and client. In the words of Stern (1997): "The availability of narratives—what we might call the 'vocabulary' of narrative—is the province of the social discourses, or cultural contexts, in which we live, and which shape us. One might even say that cultures *are* vocabularies of narrative [italics in original]" (134).

GUIDELINES FOR THE CONSTRUCTION OF NEW MEANING

ACCORDING TO RUBIN (1997), "anything goes" cannot be the rule for the construction of new meaning. Although frameworks for this are not yet fully articulated, there are at least some considerations that should be taken into account in creating a concordance through client–therapist dialogue. New meaning created in psychotherapy should be guided by the assumption that a complex, multifaceted identity will be more serviceable to the client when dealing with the environment external to treatment. Mere novelty or capriciousness in the meaning content has no place in the therapeutic setting, but neither does rigidity in adherence to commonly accepted cultural prescriptions. As Stern (1997) has noted, psychotherapists "have no choice but to be critics of the cultures within which they move and work" (141).

Some other guidelines for dealing with the content of psychotherapy can be proposed:

1. The absence of known universal truth requires the clinician to pay careful attention to the ethics and values of the mental health professions, particularly those dealing with self-determination.
2. Understanding treatment as creating new meaning requires taking very seriously the client's goals for treatment.
3. The absence of a known truth also means that the content cannot be guided by a correspondence to that truth, but the story(ies) of the client's identity should nevertheless conform to matters of known facts, such as birth dates, family composition, places of residence, illnesses, and so on.
4. Newly created meaning should be informed by and consonant with the best available understanding of human development and functioning.
5. Since the client's identity is in narrative form, attention must be paid to the coherence of that narrative and its ability to explain the client's experiences in ways that are compatible with the perspectives of both client and therapist.

6. The client's narrative should be sufficiently anchored in the broader meaning system of his or her cultural surround to be plausible to the client and others in his or her social world.

7. The narrated identity created should have some utility for the client's functioning and self-esteem in his or her social milieu.

8. The narrated identity should enhance the client's capacity for intimacy with others.

9. The identity created should help the client recognize behavioral choices that are a better fit with his or her goals.

10. The identity created should bring out existing but dormant abilities in the client such that he or she can grow in desired ways.

In utilizing these guidelines, it is important to remember that the client's story and the therapeutic concordance are not constructed all of one piece, but are constructed, deconstructed, and reconstructed in a number of sessions spread out over a period of time. It is likely that not all the achievements implied in the guidelines will be relevant to any one client. Ordinarily, therapeutic sessions have time intervals between them, and in these time intervals the client has an opportunity to test out the fit between the features of the identity and his or her life circumstances, demands, and ambitions in order to make needed adjustments. It should be expected that the dialogic process will often require a period of months, and perhaps years, in order to be complete and effective. For some clients, treatment may involve breaks of time between courses of treatment and returns to further therapeutic efforts at points of increased or different life demands.

———

Ben, a man now in his late forties, first contacted me a number of years ago regarding depression following the breakup of his second marriage. Before this marriage, Ben had participated in two years of psychotherapy in which he had spent considerable time focusing on the events of his childhood and their effects on him. An only child, he was eighteen months old when his mother committed suicide. Following his mother's death, he was placed in an orphanage until he was five or six, when his paternal grandparents took him to live with them. Eventually, his father also lived in the household for a time, but Ben was raised primarily by his grandparents, with the father playing a minor role. There was no contact with the mother's family following her death, and since his father and his grandparents never talked about her, he had little knowledge of her or of why she had taken her life. By the time Ben had entered therapy for the first time and begun questioning the effects of the early events on his personality, his father and grandparents were deceased, leaving him with no one to ask about the circumstances of his childhood.

Ben described himself as a frightened and lonely child who somehow endured what he recalled as humiliation, neglect, and abuse such as having his mouth literally washed out with soap by the nuns at the orphanage. He could not understand why his father and his grandfather cared so little about him as to allow him to remain there for such a long time. His isolated existence continued after his stay at the orphanage, since his father was peripheral in his life and his grandparents were too old to have much energy to devote to a young boy. The grandfather had built a special room for Ben in the basement, and there the latency-aged Ben spent many long hours involved in amassing various collections and learning about a range of scientific and artistic pursuits.

Ben saw his current life as having some similarities to that time. He now earned a living in a middle-management job in which he was neither invested nor particularly successful, but at which he went through the motions competently, just as he had gone through the motions to meet other's demands of him in his early school years. But, just as he had come alive only in the basement pursuits of his childhood, Ben's real emotional investment as an adult was in artistic endeavors outside work.

Ben is a very articulate and introspective man who relies on this ability in his art. Yet as he talks, at times the words themselves take over and he becomes lost in them. At such times. he continues to provide intricate descriptions of events and their presumed meaning, but he no longer knows if these words really capture his experience of himself or if they fit well only with one another and present an interesting image of common human dilemmas. At these times, then, the structure of his inner dialogue with himself collapses, and he no longer has enough ability to put distance between himself as the narrator of his stories and himself as the protagonist. He needs to have an external participant in the dialogue in order to use it reflexively.

When I saw Ben for the first time, I could hear his previous therapist's utilization of separation-individuation theory as he recounted his story. He talked of his mother's death having detracted from his participating normally in a "love affair with the world" that should have occurred at eighteen months. Ben believed that the experience of his mother's death had left him with a certain passivity in relation to interactions with others, in both his job and his relationships with women. In fact, his wife had wanted him to give up his artistic pursuits and to devote himself more single-mindedly to providing her with the economic security she craved largely because of the effects of her own deprived childhood. Although Ben had thought his wife's wishes legitimate, he had found himself reluctant to give up his art, at which, although it was not sufficient to earn him a living, he had achieved considerable recognition. He thought of his reluctance in this regard as a pathological manifestation of his passivity and an outgrowth of his activities in the basement, which he construed as an unhealthy defense against the problems in his family.

I found Ben to be an articulate and engaging man who, although certainly depressed, manifested more initiative, creativity, and social skill in our interactions than I would have expected if I had paid attention only to his description of himself. On the basis of this observation and with Winnicott's (1975b) ideas about creativity emerging from a transitional process, I suggested to him that his activity in the basement did not strike me as pathological, but as the creative manner in which he had managed to survive the difficulty of his childhood circumstances. Thus I suggested that his resistance to his wife's requests to give up his cherished art work could be understood not as a manifestation of pathological passivity, but as a healthy insistence on retaining the creative parts of himself. Over time and in part out of my suggestions, we agreed that his problem was not how to give up art, but how to bring significant others into that world so that he would not have to remain as lonely as an adult as he had been as a child.

As Ben became more invested in including others in his previously more solitary pursuits, he also became more curious about the facts of the people in his past. At one point, therefore, he obtained his mother's death certificate and was amazed at the date. He had, in fact, not been eighteen months old, as he had believed, but more than four years old. This meant that, although his memory of the time in the orphanage was that it had been interminable, the time he had actually been there had to have been considerably less than a year. Following this discovery, Ben talked more of his ideas about what being without a mother had been like for him. A mother, he concluded, was someone "who kept you in her head" all the time, confirming thereby that your existence was significant to someone.

As this therapy progressed, I noticed that although Ben had dated a number of women briefly, he was often referring indirectly to one woman he was seeing. When asked, however, Ben insisted that Lucy was not really important to him. Soon after this, he told me that he wanted to terminate our work together in a few weeks. I suggested that ending at this time was premature, but Ben refused even to consider this. When I learned that he also intended to break off his relationship with Lucy at the same time, I began to understand that it was important for Ben to leave the women in his life rather than have them leave him. I then believed both that Ben needed to do this and that he would in time return.

About a year after Ben first terminated with me, he called to say that a new play of his was being presented and it was about his treatment with me, something that was not surprising since I knew that all his work had an autobiographical element. He wanted me to see the play, after which he wanted to come back to discuss our work together. I did see the production and found that part of it involved a discussion with a therapist about the need of one of the characters to break up with a woman. Ben had also asked Lucy to see the production, and after she did they became reinvolved in their relationship. He and I also started meeting again, and this lasted for four to five months, during which time I came to believe that the premature termination had served as a test to see whether Lucy and I would be able to keep him alive in our heads. Termination this time felt comfortable.

Some four to five years later, Ben contacted me for a third time. He was now living with Lucy and said, "There have been people in my life who have loved me, but this is the first time I have been able to love someone back." The problem now was that within the next year or so Lucy's work would require her to move elsewhere, and she wanted him to go with her. He wanted to do so, but was not sure if he would be able to sustain his work and his self-image if he moved. He alluded to his anger at and fear of powerful women, and he did not want these feelings to ruin a wonderful relationship. He would lose a lot of his artistic connections if he left the city, but he thought he could manage that all right. He worried that his fear and anger might ruin the relationship, particularly if he had relatively few other friends in his life. If he could not retain a good sense of himself, he would psychologically not be able to sustain his love for Lucy. This relationship had been so special that he would rather just not go with her than have to live through the pain of watching it die.

Ben did go with Lucy when she had to move, and to my knowledge things have gone well. He has said that this time, at least, if the relationship fails he will know that it was their mutual failure and not just his alone.*

——————

I have no information about Ben's first therapy experience other than what he told me, but I know that he experienced it as useful. At that time, he was only beginning to think seriously about the meaning of his mother's suicide for his life. It is my impression that putting into words his loneliness, dealing with his difficulties in intimate relationships, and facing his sense of a passive relationship with his environment were a part of his concerns as he entered that treatment. The concordance that he and his therapist created utilized Mahlerian (Mahler, Pine, and Bergman 1975) separation-individuation theory to understand these difficulties and to help Ben achieve a sense that these problems could be overcome. He believed that he would never have married for the second time had he not had this therapy.

Unfortunately, his wife—whom he chose in part because of her ability to understand his childhood problems—had her own issues from her childhood, and she left the marriage when Ben could not provide her with the financial security she wanted. After the end of this marriage, Ben's previous understanding that he had difficulties as a result of his childhood only contributed to a sense that the failure was inevitable due to his pathologic need to continue his isolated artistic activities. The concordance that had been useful could no longer be useful. Thus it was necessary to examine his past from a different theoretical lens that could be useful in explaining why he needed to hold onto his artistic endeavors. Winnicott's (1971a) theory of transitional phenomena and creativity was an obvious alternative. The work with Ben, therefore, is a good example of the human need continually to retell, revise, and rewrite the

———————————————————————————————

*This case was previously discussed in C. Saari, "Intersubjectivity, language, and culture: Bridging the person/environment gap?" *Smith College Studies in Social Work* 69 (1998): 221–237.

stories that constitute individual identity. (The case also provides—in Ben's ability to love Lucy after she and I had passed the test of being able to hold him in mind—a good illustration of the relevance of Benjamin's [1988] theory of recognition.)

In Ben's internal life, there was considerable conflict about women, whom he saw both as potential caretakers for whom he longed and as potentially devastating, in that their abandonment after seducing him into a relationship seemed inevitable. He also had many impressions of his childhood experience that he could not put into words. Thus we can say that he had uninterpreted unconscious meanings that needed to be understood. It is my impression that his first therapy dealt more with this kind of unconscious than did his work with me, although this certainly was part of what we did. However, I was always more impressed with Ben's facility with words to express potential meaning and his becoming lost in the verbiage. Ben would almost always have something he wanted to talk about when he came to therapy and would describe and then analyze this topic in depth. Yet if I asked him what all that meant to him, he would often be at a loss for words. On balance, he and I focused more on his unintegrated unconscious.

Schafer (1983) has emphasized that one of the important results of analysis is that the person not only should experience life and its complexity more vividly, but also should be able to take ownership of his or her history and its influence in the present. Certainly, Ben, as narrator, needed to understand how his protagonist had been affected by his mother's suicide and its aftermath in order to take ownership of these effects in his present life. Yet as the narrator of the present, he also needed to be able to convey his experiences to others in words that would have affective meaning to him and to those others. There is reason to believe that his writing about his experience in therapy and having this performed with both Lucy and me present enabled him to connect his verbal rendering of the experience and his current internal state in a way that made the words have the affective resonance to which they supposedly pertained. There is, in fact, reason to think that he may have benefitted more through the premature termination and the subsequent play than he would have had he simply continued to use words in which to talk with me in a therapeutic setting. It is, however, important that following the play he did return to treatment to consider further his current construction of his identity.

The concordance that Ben and I constructed changed not only from that created with his previous therapist, but also from the new factual information that his mother's death certificate provided. The therapeutic culture needs to be responsive to knowledge about the environment as it relates to both the client's goals and the known circumstances of the client's life. Understanding the client's environment can both open up new possibilities for narrative construction and put some limitations on possibilities for construction, the latter due to the necessity that the story be credible. In Ben's case, part of the credibility stemmed from the story's having many elements consonant with culturally sanctioned themes about the life of the struggling artist, and it was in such themes that the concordance and his identity were housed.

EIGHT / THE IMPORTANCE OF RELATIONSHIPS

ALTHOUGH FREUD PAID some attention to the therapeutic relationship, he saw the development of insight and rationality,
acquired through the analyst's interpretations, as the curative
element in psychoanalysis. Yet in recent years, an emphasis on the therapeutic relationship has moved to the center of theoretical considerations. In 1995, Schafer noted that although conceptions of dialogue and
intersubjectivity differed, they were pervading the psychoanalytic literature on therapeutic action. Mitchell (1993:37) has observed that
patients do not hear interpretations as interpretations, but as relational
events. At another point Mitchell remarks, "That which is most deeply
personal is often arrived at only through interaction" (35). Within psychoanalysis, of course, there has always been an interpersonal school,
identified mostly with Sullivan and his followers, but until recently this
school remained outside the mainstream of psychoanalytic theory
(Hirsch 1998). As is now often observed, psychoanalytic theory has
moved from the "myth of the isolated mind" (Stolorow and Atwood
1992:7–28) to an acknowledgment of a two-person interacting system.
The human environment is being taken seriously.

Clinical social work, in contrast to psychoanalysis, has traditionally
considered the client–therapist relationship to be crucial for treatment
success. During the 1940s and 1950s, virtually every major social work
theoretician discussed the concept of relationship, so much so in fact
that Perlman (1979) suggested that it was "discussed to death" (15).
Biestek (1994) observed that the importance of the relationship is uni-
versally recognized and called the relationship "the soul of casework"
(630). More recently, Hartman (1988) noted that there are many differences in points of view among social workers, but that the perspective
of the person-in-environment and the view that change takes place
within the context of a relationship are common to all. Currently in
social work literature, however, there has been a tendency to take

the importance of the relationship for granted, an attitude that is particularly striking when taken in comparison with current psychoanalytic discourse.

Chapter 1 discussed attachment theory, originated by Bowlby (1969) and beginning with observations of autistic-like behavior in institutionalized infants who had little interaction with human beings, which was disdained for some years by psychoanalytic theorists as too biological. Yet attachment theory, too, has received considerable attention in the current literature, largely because of evidence that the young brain needs interactions with the environment in order to develop proper neurological functioning. Of additional importance are a number of longitudinal studies (Hamilton 2000; Waters, Hamilton, and Weinfield 2000; Waters, Merrick, et al. 2000; Weinfield, Sroufe, and Egeland 2000) indicating that about 73 percent of children classified for styles of attachment in toddlerhood remained in the same classification group at adolescence or early adulthood. The approximately 27 percent of the cases in which attachment patterns had changed seemed related to the impact of significant negative life experiences at some later point in childhood.

Relationship patterns established in childhood, therefore, seem to become part of the implicit-memory system that underlies human interactions throughout life. Such patterns appear not to be totally unchangeable, although some resistance to change should be expected. In regard to the significance of attachment patterns to psychotherapy, Amini and colleagues (1996) have said:

> From a psychobiologic viewpoint, psychotherapy is not merely a conversation, or an intellectual exchange of words and ideas. Instead, it is an attachment relationship, which is a physiologic process capable of regulating neurophysiology and altering underlying neural structure. From this perspective, the effectiveness of psychotherapy is owed to its ability to engage and direct this phylogenetically ancient mechanism. From this perspective, psychotherapy is just as "biological" as any other treatment modality. (232)

Amini and co-workers, however, note that "in order for implicit affective learning to take place, the patient must have a vivid affective experience of the therapist" (234). Geller's (1998) research reports have also used the term *vivid* to describe the finding that patients who experienced

the most benefit from their treatment also had stable internal representations of their therapists and carried on internal conversations with
them long after the treatment had terminated.

While there is now much agreement that the psychotherapist cannot
simply be a "blank screen," there is also much debate about what the
nature of the psychotherapeutic relationship ought to be (Goldstein
1994; Hirsch 1998; Raines 1996; Renik 1993, 1997). Under what circumstances should a therapist reveal something about him- or herself?
What can safely be revealed? What should be concealed? Aron (1996:
228) has emphasized that self-revelation is not a choice, but an in-
evitability in treatment. Aron has also said: "*If in the classical model the
idea is to be analyzed well enough to keep one's own problems out of the
way, in a relational model, I suggest, the analyst needs to be analyzed
well enough to tolerate some degree of anxiety about having a good deal
of his or her character exposed and scrutinized by patients* [italics in
original]" (249). Lomas (1990) put this more personally:

> The rule of abstinence presents a particular kind of temptation to
> the therapist: a withdrawal into a safe, narcissistic cocoon. Practi-
> tioners are in a very vulnerable position. When I think of the messes
> I have made—and continue to make—in my own life I wonder that
> I have the audacity to invite people into my consulting room and set
> myself up as someone who may help them. I know that, come what
> may, I try to present myself as wiser and more serene than I believe
> myself to be. To some extent I do this in order to engender confi-
> dence and to spare them a too sudden and radical disillusionment;
> but to a large extent I do it to satisfy my own needs. I want them to
> think of me as above serious criticism. If, however, the temptation
> for the therapist to withdraw into narcissism is increased by a the-
> ory that encourages and validates this stance, then we are indeed in
> trouble. (68)

FROM ACTING-OUT TO ENACTMENT

FREUD BELIEVED THAT affects and actions distorted reality, especially the reality of the transference, and thought that words were more
capable of capturing unconscious meaning (Saari 1986, 1988; Schimek
1975). Thus, for Freud, actions within therapy constituted acting-out

and should be avoided. Current developmental theory, however, views action rather than language as primary. Piaget (1962) proposed that infants begin with inborn action patterns such as sucking, which become activated by contact with the external world. Action patterns, according to Piaget, can be modified in each encounter with the environment, through processes he termed *assimilation* and *accommodation*, and can then be integrated with all past encounters. Thus in Piaget's theory, even the unconscious patterning that we now call implicit memory can conceivably be altered through current experience. It is, therefore, at least possible that patterns of interaction with human others can be altered in interactions with a therapist, even in the absence of any interpretation or verbal recognition of this change. It is likely, however, that the activity of relating to another human being in one's immediate environment—part of what Bronfenbrenner (1999) calls *proximal processes*—can be altered, although only within actions that occur on a regular basis and over an extensive period of time.

Loewald, while believing that actions are important in treatment, thought that ordinarily it is important to put actions into words for the patient, but he saw the actions as likely to come first. In "Psychoanalysis as an Art and the Fantasy Character of the Psychoanalytic Situation" (1980d), he used the analogy of a drama to describe analytic process. The patient is the author; the analyst is the stage director; both act out the various parts, switching roles at points in the play; but it is essential that both periodically step back from the action to become drama critics. Schafer (1983), in agreement with Loewald, noted that patients not only tell us about their problems, but also show us. In recent years, however, the idea that patient and therapist are likely to "enact" between them aspects of the patient's experience (and at least potentially of the therapist's as well) has become common within the literature, particularly in that of the relational school.

Freud also wanted his theory to be scientific, and he created his theory within what he understood to be an appropriately causal framework. As such, meanings were caused by the motivational patterns of the inherited unconscious. Bruner (1986), however, has since pointed out that there are two basic modes of thinking. The causal framework, which Bruner calls "paradigmatic," deals with predictions and attempts to isolate those elements that are necessary and sufficient to cause something regardless of its context. The meaning framework, however, deals with the creation of a narrative that is only one of many possible ways in which something could have occurred, must be formulated on an ex post facto basis, and is invariably context dependent. Within a postmodern frame of reference, of course, psychotherapy is concerned with meanings, primarily in the form of narratives. Thus, in therapy, interpretation deals with the meaning of events that have occurred and cannot be made until after the action of the event.

Enactment, or actions that occur unconsciously between therapist and patient and that are related to past experience of the patient, but sometimes also of the therapist, is increasingly discussed in psychoanalytic literature. While some theorists regard enactments as isolated events within the treatment, others, such as Renik (1997) and Friedman and Natterson (1999), see enactment as occurring continually. Renik has commented, "We can only see ourselves in the rearview mirror"(282). Hirsch (1996) suggests that there needs to be a switch from seeing the therapist as a "participant-observer" to seeing her as an "observing participant." There is a recognition here that the psychotherapist is not able to remain outside the therapy processes and does not have a superior view of reality. Rather, to put this into the terms of Loewald's (1980d) play analogy, the therapist is a more experienced drama critic than is the patient. Aron (1996:28) points out that what is meant by "analytic neutrality" must be seen as the therapist's openness to new perspectives, his commitment to taking other perspectives seriously, and his refusal to accept anything as the final answer.

Of course, viewing psychotherapeutic processes as involving the creation of meaning in the present rather than the discovery of past events and meanings alters the understanding of how psychotherapy helps. Treatment is not expected to uncover the ultimate answer to the client's problems, but to help the client accept, enhance, and appreciate his or her inner experience as well as his or her enjoyment of the external world and the life that the environment makes possible. There is no attempt to rid oneself of reality-distorting affect, but to tolerate one's emotions (Krystal 1988; Zetzel 1970) and to learn to understand them as crucially important information about self and environment.

The relationship between self and environment is also viewed differently within this approach to treatment. Stern (1997) notes that we must accept and take seriously the embeddedness of our experience in culture and in relationships. Rubin (1997) points out that most contemporary psychoanalytic theorists believe that the healthy human being is interdependent and inextricably bound to family, society, and culture. Rubin further comments, "Of greater significance is the realization that civilization is not imposed on basic human nature, but part of the fabric of nature itself" (6). As was pointed out in part 1, human beings define their very identity in terms of their comprehension of their environment but need interactions with other humans in order to create this identity. The work with Catherine, described in the following case, illustrates this.

Catherine was a thirty-nine-year-old accountant, a single woman employed full time by a prominent and publicly renowned family to handle some of their financial affairs. A strikingly beautiful woman, she initially appeared poised and quite competent. She asked for help with depression, panic attacks, and her difficulty in getting along with her mother. She was also concerned that she had no intimate relationship and no children. She had been referred to me by a colleague who had treated her in her late twenties and with whom she had maintained contact through holiday cards after he moved out of town. In talking with me about her, he said, "She's a perfect client to have in a private practice. She comes regularly; she pays on time; she never bothers you between sessions; but I am not sure she does much in the sessions either."

In her second session, Catherine indicated that she had no close friends and did not know how to meet people. She was invited relatively frequently to parties, but the people there never were really interested in her. When I asked how she knew this, she said as soon as they found out what she did, they just wanted to hear about that—not about her. I then asked what people would ask her about if they really were interested in her. Her reply, that she did not know, came after some moments of thought, and it told me that she could not see her professional success as being part of herself.

For the first several months, Catherine did indeed come regularly. She talked about her life, but did not want me to say anything at all; in fact, she would cut me off if I attempted to say anything. After a few sessions of this, I began feeling negated and, after about four months, began wondering what she was getting out of the therapy and whether I was simply exploiting this woman who came, paid, and yet seemed to do little that was likely to be of much help to her. I decided, therefore, to comment on her seeming not to want me to say anything and ask how she understood this. Catherine seemed panicked, "What's the matter? You like me don't you? You want me to come to see you?" I explained that I did want to help her, but did not know how to understand her apparent wish for me not to talk.

Catherine then explained that she was very serious about this therapy and really wanted it to be helpful. Yet if she got to know anything about me, she would have to care about and take care of me and that was not what she wanted: she wanted help for herself. Catherine's answers about this helped me realize that, for her, only one person in any relationship could be taken care of. She literally had no conception or expectation of mutuality in relationships. I tried to convey to her that I also wanted this therapy to be useful to her, but that she would have to help me understand what she was saying and that sometimes that meant that I would have to clarify something she had said or make some comment on how I understood it. Additionally, I needed to know if she was experiencing our relationship as helpful to her or not. Catherine said she would try to allow for this, but mostly seemed puzzled.

Catherine, as I was learning, had four alcoholic grandparents, an alcoholic father, and a mother with diabetes. Her understanding of what determined the nature of human interactions was that this literally depended on what substances the person had in their blood at the time. She was the oldest of four siblings and, since both her parents were working, had taken over the care of the younger children at a very early age. If the other children got into trouble or did something wrong, it was (at least according to her experience) she who was blamed.

The father, who was apparently not a mean drunk, would give her special attention when he was inebriated, and she had longed for his affection, but he rarely actually did the things he promised when he had been drinking. Toward the end of her father's life, when he no longer could work well for anyone else, the family had bought a large apartment building and the father was renovating it and turning it into condominiums. Each of the family members was given an apartment to keep for him- or herself. Catherine had envisioned the family all living together, but in separate units, and saw this as almost a utopian existence. In the end, however, the father died of cirrhosis of the liver before the building was complete, and only Catherine had actually moved into her unit—a major disappointment for her.

About three weeks after I asked about why it was important to her for me to be silent, Catherine asked if I liked coffee, pointing out that she liked to have a cup about the time of our appointment. Would I like her to bring me coffee? I wondered if this would not be her taking care of me, something she had not wanted to do. She assured me that this would be all right and that she wanted to do it. I therefore agreed. What ensued was something like a Japanese tea ceremony, with Catherine's sessions beginning with her handing out the coffee as well as sugar and cream, and the two of us settling into our accustomed places to begin the hour. It was an activity that confirmed our relatedness to each other.

Several months later, Catherine had an accident in which she broke a leg. She called and that said she would be unable to attend sessions for several weeks. Then she phoned to say that she would be able to come again, but was still on crutches, and so I should not be surprised if she was a little late. On the particular day, I had no appointment right before Catherine's and decided to go to the coffee shop in the building's lobby to get us coffee about fifteen minutes before she was to arrive, thinking that Catherine would be unable to do this. As I disembarked from the elevator, there was Catherine, leaning up against the wall and looking exhausted, a bag with the coffee dangling from one crutch handle. Confused at seeing me there, Catherine said, "You didn't forget, did you? You knew I was coming?" I told her of my intention to get us coffee.

My determination to do this very small thing for Catherine created a shift in our relationship, enabling her to see me as caring for her in a way she had not expected. Although she continued to have serious difficulties in relatedness with others, this did help to move her a little toward expecting mutuality.

—————

Although I cannot connect the coffee incident to any particular previous experience of Catherine's, it is clear that this was an enactment related to what she had come to understand human relationships to be like. It should also be pointed out that there was very little verbalization between us regarding our relationship—either at the beginning of the coffee ceremony or at the time of her needing to come on crutches. Indeed, I suspect that, for Catherine, to point out shifts in our relationship verbally would have been likely to diminish the effect of the experience for her. There are times when shared experiences should be honored nonverbally rather than analyzed away. Loewald (1980b) pointed out that part of what psychotherapy offers a patient is a new relationship within which that person can reexperience and perhaps alter the previously constructed patterns through which relationships are enacted.

Geller (1998), whose research on patients' representations of their therapists has found that people who see the treatment as helpful carry on internal dialogues with their therapist long after the termination of the treatment, has said:

> The research we have conducted underscores the feasibility and importance of also studying the ways in which patients interact with the felt presence of their therapists between sessions, during vacations, and after termination. Furthermore, the accumulating findings lend support to the hypothesis that there is clinical value in devoting increased attention to the interpersonal and experiential learning that takes place while patients and therapists are pursuing the definable projects that characterize particular approaches to therapy. (210)

As Geller suggests, however, the therapeutic relationship does not and should not consist simply of "hanging out" with the client or displaying a generalized unconditional positive regard.

THE THERAPEUTIC ENVIRONMENT

THERAPIST–PATIENT INTERACTIONS must involve some kind of content, and that content is the patient's life experience along with attitudes about these experiences; however, the importance of what occurs may not be the literal meaning of the content. Pizer (1996) has pointed out that newer perspectives, particularly the relational perspective, are causing shifts in the understanding of what is important in psychoanalytic interactions:

> Another implication for clinical technique is the shift in emphasis from content to the patient's state while communicating content. States, state shifts, and negotiated state transitions more centrally

occupy the analyst's attention as well as the relational process. To whatever degree these state shifts are, or are not, talked about, they are *lived* between the analytic partners. And this living out, with all its struggles and negotiations, increasingly carries the therapeutic action [italics in original]. (505)

The patient's state, however, can be seen to be reactive to at least three factors (in addition to physiological state): the degree of comfort in the external setting; the degree of conflict, shame, or guilt that is experienced in relation to the life experience under consideration; and, finally, the degree of comfort in discussing this content with the therapist, which may also be seen as the nature of the therapist–client relationship.

In general, it appears that most therapists think of Winnicott's (1986) "holding environment" or Bion's (1962) "containment" as the degree of comfort supplied by the presence of the therapist. Yet the features of the nonhuman setting in which the treatment interactions take place also make a difference. Ordinarily, it has been thought that the therapist's office ought to convey a sense of soothing qualities in objects that do not suggest specific meanings but allow for a wide variety of tastes. It must, after all, be a place where many people with differing problems can be comfortable, and paying attention to how an office's furnishings will be seen by various groups of people can make a difference. For example, if the waiting room has no magazines that target a minority population, people of that minority may not feel very welcome. The therapist's taste and comfort, however, may often be important determinants of the nature of the office decor, and this is certainly a legitimate consideration since the therapist must be able to be sufficiently comfortable to focus on the client's states and needs rather than on her own.

There are, however, times when therapeutic interactions would be advantaged by taking place elsewhere. Some people with agoraphobia, for example, are best seen in the spaces to which they have confined themselves in order to help them reflect on their experience in other environments usefully. In work with potentially violent patients, interactions must occur where both patient and therapist can be assured of the nearby presence of others who can intervene should any difficulties arise. Anxious adolescents often talk more freely when on walks through the neighborhood. Sometimes the therapy may involve the client's participation in an activity, and a discussion of that activity may best be held where it takes place. For example, many years ago I was assigned by an agency to visit the home of a woman who had just given birth to an infant who, although healthy, had no eyeballs. At the woman's home, I observed that when she fed the baby, which she did at regular intervals, she acted as if, because the infant could not open his eyes, there was no difference for him between sleeping and waking states; she thus gave him no time to wake up if he had been sleeping. Had I not been able to see the manner in which this very distressed mother altered her care of her blind child from the manner in which she had cared for her older, sighted child, I think it unlikely that she and I would have been able to deal with the crisis that she and her child were undergoing. One might almost say that I was purposely using the home environment in order to have access to enactments. The point here is that there may be good reasons to choose to interact with a patient in an environment other than the therapist's office.

Often practicality is an overriding factor in determining the nature of the environment of the therapy setting. A therapist who has to travel distances to see patients in settings other than the office will not be able to see as many patients as one who stays in the same place and the patients do the traveling. However, it is important to realize that the setting of the four walls of an office is not a crucial element in treatment effectiveness. The use of an office may at times protect the therapist from having to reveal aspects of herself by its protecting anonymity, but sometimes treatment can be more effective if it takes place elsewhere.

The second factor influencing the client's state is his or her comfort or discomfort with the content under discussion. Some content areas are often uncomfortable for clients to discuss—sexual activities, for example. There are, however, wide variations among people in the affective tone that accompanies any topic, and this is based on individual experience. Individual experience is, however, always blended with cultural factors—values, norms, ways of problem solving, and behaviors that are either highly prescribed or highly proscribed. Thus the union between individual and cultural experience is always seamless. Here it is important to remember that the client's identity has been constructed through event representations and that the experience of self involves "what it is like to be me" in various environments; what it is like to be me in therapy is one of the environments.

The third influence on the client's state is his or her comfort with the therapist in discussing the particular content—that is, the nature of the relationship. Benjamin's (1988, 1998, 1999) understanding of human relationships is particularly interesting in this regard. She begins with Winnicott's (1971b) idea that the infant, out of his or her omnipotence, must psychologically "destroy" the caretaking person out of "hate" at the caretaker's failure to meet all needs. When both caretaker and infant survive the destruction, the infant comes to realize that the caretaker is a separate person with a separate mind with whom interactions are possible. Benjamin builds on Winnicott here, noting that when the infant has experienced the survival of the other, the infant then seeks recognition from that surviving, independent other, and the capacity for mutual sharing with another is born. Note that there are many clients, like Catherine, for whom childhood conditions make it impossible to engage in a cycle of destruction, survival, and recognition. It is not that the therapy relationship entered into by clients like Catherine is not important, for, indeed, with these clients the relationship is absolutely critical. Rather, the relationship cannot yet bear the strain of difference, negotiation, anger, or intimacy.

Notable for the theme of this book, Benjamin (1999) also sees the ongoing human process of destruction and recognition as a dialectic between fantasy and external reality. About this, she says: "This reality principle does not represent a detour to wish fulfillment, a modification of the pleasure principle. Nor is it the acceptance of a false life of adaptation. Rather it is a continuation under more complex conditions of the infant's original fascination with and love of what is outside, his appreciation of difference and novelty" (193). The implication, of course, is that there is a connection between positive interactions with human others and an enjoyment of the nonhuman external world, something that was observed to be the case many years ago in the hospitalism studies (e.g., Spitz 1965). Sadly, clients like Catherine are stuck in a bleak world with little capacity for fantasy, illusion, or play.

TRACKING THE CLIENT'S INNER STATE

WINNICOTT (1958; SAARI 1991) proposed that in significant relationships human beings cannot function when fused psychologically with another person or when in psychological isolation from others. Love for another brings one psychologically closer to the loved person, thereby reducing the psychological space between self and other. Being in a closer relationship to another person, however, increases the intensity of any emotion the person might feel (not just the affection for the other person). If there is too much closeness, the increase in emotional experience may become threatening, and the possibility of diffusion or fragmentation of the self is raised, stimulating the person to seek more distance from the interacting other. Anger or hate increases the interpsychic distance and helps to consolidate a sense of an intact and energized self. However, too much anger or hate brings with it the threat of isolation and/or exhaustion. People are, therefore, always having to negotiate the relative degree of closeness or distance between themselves and the significant other with whom they are interacting. Yet how much closeness or distance can be tolerated also varies with different people. Those whose interpersonal experiences have involved warmth and attention to their needs are more likely to want and tolerate more closeness than people who have found that openness to relationships with others ends in disappointment and pain. These people can also tolerate more affect without acting on it in an impulsive or a destructive manner.

The concept of interpsychic space can be used as a conceptual way to link the complex and changing relationships among person, situation, and an interacting other (note that these are also the three elements in Winnicott's [1975b] transitional process). It has already been pointed out that the person and the situation are linked through the evaluation of the safety of the self in that situation provided through affective/cognitive processes (Basch 1976). However, the person's evaluation of the situation also affects the degree of interpsychic space needed between the self and the interacting partner, with conditions seen as safe allowing for more interpsychic closeness and conditions seen as threatening requiring more interpsychic distance. Observing the interrelationships and shifts among these three factors in treatment processes can be very useful to an attempt at providing the level of connectedness the client needs throughout the session.

———

Phoebe, a twenty-four-year-old woman, began therapy shortly after moving to a new geographical area with the idea of seeking to live her life away from her family and to learn more about herself apart from them. The youngest of three children (she had two older brothers), Phoebe was only five years old when her father committed suicide. The father had been very unstable—a drug addict and a gambler. Following the father's death, Phoebe's mother had held two jobs in order to provide for herself and her children. During this time, Phoebe was cared for mostly by her elder brother, who at the time of this session was himself a recovering drug addict. Phoebe had a particularly conflicted relationship with this brother.

The session under consideration occurred about six months into treatment and at a time when a comfortable working relationship with me appeared to have been established. The session reported here also occurred at a time when there was only one more scheduled session before my vacation was to begin. Ordinarily, Phoebe had been very involved in treatment, usually arriving with things she wanted to discuss either from the last week's discussion or from her week. It had also been characteristic of her to want perfection from herself and often from others.

As she enters the office, Phoebe is carrying an ice cream sundae and comments, "I'm treating myself tonight. Sorry, I didn't bring you one." The tone of the second sentence does not indicate an apology, but points out to me that the decision not to bring me one was consciously intentional. (I know that Phoebe is pushing me away, but I do not yet know why: perhaps the coming vacation is creating a need for her to feel more self-reliant; hence the treatment environment feels less safe than usual. Or perhaps something else has occurred.)

Sitting down, Phoebe uncharacteristically remarks that she had not wanted to come today. She is, she says, very busy at work on an important project and needs to devote all her attention to it. She is, however, doing very well on the project, and today her boss, who rarely compliments anyone, told her she was doing a great job. That's why she is treating herself to the sundae. I indicate an interest in the project that is so important, and Phoebe begins to tell me about it. (I still do not know what is happening here, but know that she is very invested in her career and ordinarily gains pleasure from experiencing herself as competent. I am still not sure why she is needing to bolster her feeling of competence, but assume that there is some reason for this, which may become apparent if I listen carefully.)

Having explained in some detail her work, Phoebe becomes silent for a time. Then, with a much lower and more hesitating voice, she says, "My brother was in town this weekend. That's really why I did not want to come here today." She then tells me of the difficult time she had with her brother and, tearfully, of her fears that he might someday kill himself, as did her father. She is not sure she could survive the brother's committing suicide. (Having experienced herself as a competent person and being recognized by me for this, Phoebe feels strong enough to tell me of the major reason she had been feeling vulnerable when she came in—something she feels so strongly that she otherwise perhaps could not have psychologically survived telling me about.) The rest of the session consists of a discussion of the weekend and her concerns about her brother.

In leaving, Phoebe asks me the name of a plant in the office. I tell her, and she comments that it is pretty: "I haven't noticed that before. I guess when I am here I am usually just looking at that horrible fern." I ask what it is about the fern she does not like. "Look at it! It's half dead and half alive." To me the fern is not half dead, but, as it is sitting on a bookcase on the wall, it grows only in one direction. (Phoebe must now go out into the world in which she has to meet others' demands on her as well as her own rather harsh ones, so she must consolidate her sense of self by increasing the interpsychic space between us. The issue of death, of course, she will take with her, and I wonder if she sometimes experiences herself as half dead and half alive. For sure, however, I am only half helpful, and the issue of the vacation is still there.)

———

In spite of her family's problems, Phoebe is relatively healthy, and it is possible to see her modulating the interpsychic space between us as our interactions take place and her affective/cognitive state shifts. In contrast, Catherine maintains considerable distance in interpsychic space, and there appear to be few modulations. Catherine cannot react in different ways to different environments and she thereby protects herself from pain, but also from intimacy and enjoyment when the environment offers these possibilities. Phoebe, although she struggles with her inner life, can allow herself to experience more pain, more pleasure, and more relatedness to others.

Interrelationships among the external environment, the interactive human other, and the internal subjective world of the individual are so complex that it is not surprising that they have been difficult to capture in any theory, and there is much conceptual work to be done in this area. However, for an observing participant in interactions with a client, there is a useful way to think about this: it involves an analogy to the physiology of the eye.* In this analogy, the retina serves as the agent through which information and affective/cognitive evaluation can be made, and the pupil acts like interpsychic space, allowing for optimal conditions for the self to operate. Interpsychic space (the pupil), however, may be changed in reaction to different conditions that may involve either the inner or the outer environment:

1. There is too much information (or too little) for the retina and the brain to process in the internal world.

2. The affective/cognitive evaluation is too painful or negative (or has become more positive), and extra effort must be made to deal with the implications for integrating this painful material into the state of the self.

3. The nature of the external environment seems less safe (or safer) than it may have earlier.

4. The person is physically tired and cannot process much more input.

Interpsychic space changes in reaction to both the internal and the external environments. That is, Phoebe can be understood to have increased the psychic distance between us in reaction to both her internal upset over her weekend with her brother and the external condition of the treatment situation seeming less comfortable because of the coming vacation. Had I chosen to focus right away on her challenges regarding our relationship (the messages that she had not brought me a sundae and that she had not wanted to come), I would have been demanding that we operate with less interpsychic space. Had I done that, however, it is quite possible that I would simply have gotten us into a covert battle over our relationship, thereby adding further to her need for more interpsychic space. Under that circumstance, I would probably never have heard about the state of her internal environment after the weekend with her brother. Tracking and respecting a client's need for an optimal degree of interpsychic space is one of the major tasks of psychotherapy and serves as a framework within which empathy can be created. However, this can be done only through taking into account both the relationship between the client and the therapist and the manner in which the client experiences the environment.

---

*I am indebted to Joseph W. Dooley for suggesting the usefulness of the analogy.

NINE / SYMBOLIZATION: CONNECTIONS BETWEEN INTERNAL AND EXTERNAL WORLDS

NELSON'S (1985) tripartite theory of meaning describes a system that consists of the communicative context of meaning, the cognitive representation of meaning, and the conventional meaning of words within the linguistic-cultural community. Earlier I dealt with the child's creation of a sense of identity by first constructing an understanding of his or her environment and then, through cognitive operations on that world, understanding his or her own place in that world. In this chapter, the focus is on the importance of the third aspect of meaning—the conventional meaning of words within the linguistic-cultural community, or, more simply, language.

Much of postmodern thinking is based on changes in the understanding of language that have occurred since Freud's time, when the most important aspect of language was considered to be a particular word's ability to represent through its pairing with a particular thing in the external world. For example, the name Pixie refers to a particular dog; yet knowing that Pixie is a dog also tells us that Pixie is a member of a four-legged animal class, *canine*, which, in turn, tells us much more: Pixie not only has four legs, but also is likely to bark, to be loyal to her human owner, to have the potential to be trained to perform useful work, and to have other characteristics of her species. The knowledge that we have about dogs, and about Pixie as an example of a dog, does not come through the isolated equation of Pixie = dog, but through the chain of related words and concepts into which Pixie as a dog is embedded. It is in this sense that Gergen (1994) and others see words as referring only to other words. Stern (1997), for example, says, "Meaning depends on the relations and differences *between* symbols, not of fixed identifications of symbols with entities" (7).

According to Nelson (1985), the fact that the semantic aspect of language is not automatically embedded into conceptual relationships is an advantage, allowing for the possibility of new and creative linkages

between ideas or objects without the more cumbersome work of access-
ing the cognitive representations of the ideas or objects. Metaphors can
be particularly useful for creating such linkages in treatment. One
client's mother, for example, kept a full candy dish in the living room for
company, but the client was forbidden ever to have any candy from that
dish or from anywhere else. The mother's rationale was that candy
would ruin her teeth. In treatment, "candy," therefore, became a shorthand way to talk about the manner in which the client felt she had been
teased with the possible availability of many different goodies that
existed in the world, but that she had always felt were denied her.

For Nelson (1985), however, once a new connection at the semantic
level has been made (i.e., candy as something desirable that is forbidden), the validity of the new relationships created must be examined
through the implications that they reflect. For example, does this
new metaphor involving candy really capture other forbidden desires
of which the client might not have been aware previously but that do
fit with her current experience of herself? Would the metaphor still
fit the client's experience if it was extended to mean "taking candy from
a baby"? In other words, does the client's meaning also extend to an
experience of herself as a baby? Thus words as used by a particular
client may or may not have many connections at the more personal
conceptual level. For example, I may be able to be quite eloquent about
the terrible living conditions existent within a slum neighborhood, but,
if I have not been there, my picture of the problems may not be very
vivid and perhaps may not even be very accurate. I can use words to talk
about slums, but these words do not have much connection at the
representational level. The recognition that words may not have such
representational capacities is also important to psychotherapists
because a client who tells us "I feel guilty" may or may not be coupling
the word *guilty* with inner experience. As was mentioned in the introduction, this lack of connection between words and feelings has been
called alexithymia.

Language, then, is of critical importance to clinical theory because
through the symbolization that language makes possible, clients can be
helped to reinterpret their experiences of both themselves and their
worlds. That language can create new possibilities through the inter-
connections between words as symbols is a major reason that interpretation, as Freud understood it and as many of his followers like him

have practiced it, has helped innumerable patients over the years. Yet because language does not automatically refer to anything other than other words, new insights received from interpretations in treatment need to be examined and integrated into other knowledge of self and world if they are to be truly mutative.

The language in which we both communicate and think is, however, inherited from the cultural community into which we are born. Language is fundamentally cultural from the outset. It involves a network of interrelated meanings that children learn as they learn how to talk, and it emphasizes particular ways of understanding what is important to notice in the world, what causal relationships and/or chains of events are expectable, and what behaviors are or are not sanctioned within that world. The young child who has acquired an event representation for what happens at a birthday party has learned that there is a category of things that can be taken to be presents. He also learns that jump ropes can belong to that category, but snakes ordinarily do not. Through their ability to be utilized and manipulated in our minds, symbols literally make connections between the external environment and the inner world (Vygotsky 1962).

Symbols are, however, social not just in the choice of symbol and its relations with other symbols, but also in the manner in which the capacity to use them is acquired. The capacity to communicate and to use symbols has its beginning with the neonate. Cavell (1993) explained:

> The infant is biologically programmed to do things that other people will interpret as meaningful signals for help. His cries are meaningful to us, but not to him. What is initially a cry without meaning to the crier, not a sign intended to be understood in a particular way, becomes meaningful in part through the behavior it produces in another. The child then begins to acquire concepts through that intercourse with other persons through which it acquires language. (223)

By about eight months, the infant can participate in the "sharing of objects of contemplation with a significant other" (Werner and Kaplan 1963:19–36), which Werner and Kaplan refer to as the contemplative situation. When an object, perhaps a toy, is attractive to the infant, and the caretaker notices the child's fascination, that caretaker might well say, "Pretty," to characterize what the adult thinks is the attractive quality of the object. Later, the child can point to the toy and say "Pretty," or some approximation thereof. The contemplative situation consists of child, a significant other, and an object in the environment. The symbol arises from the relationship among these three. As Werner and Kaplan were aware, the contemplative situation involves the same elements as those from which Winnicott (1975b) saw the transitional object arising and from which a number of psychoanalytic theorists have believed the capacity to symbolize begins (e.g., Tolpin 1971).

The symbols through which we organize our understandings of ourselves and of others, as well as the way in which we communicate to ourselves and others, are inescapably social and invariably reflective of the environment in which we live.

DIALOGUE

PSYCHOANALYTIC THEORY is, as has been noted, increasingly being seen as involving dialogue. Indeed, identity, that basic sense of who we are that guides both our sense of ourselves and our behavior, can be understood to be constituted through dialogue. Maranhao (1990) has explained: "These traits of his identity, however, do not precede dialogue; they are bestowed upon him as he speaks and listens. The subject comes into being together with dialogue and is as much a meaning-content in the process as are the things talked about" (18). Recall that not only does the patient's identity undergo evaluation and reconstruction during the therapy itself, but, as Geller (1998) has told us, patients who regard their psychotherapy as having been beneficial carry on inner dialogues with their therapists that continue long after the treatment itself has ended. Thus not only does treatment involve interpersonal interaction, but the interpersonal quality appears to continue in an inner dialogue that may well account for much of the continuing benefit of the treatment.

Mikhail Bakhtin (1981, 1990), a Russian philosopher and linguist who is considered a giant in the understanding of dialogue, pointed out that human beings need a dialogue with others in order to complete their understanding of themselves. For Bakhtin, this is a necessary and logical result of the fact that two people cannot occupy the same space. We cannot, for example, see our own face as we act and must rely on the reactions of others for information about how we appear. Thus a therapist will inevitably see a client differently than the client sees him- or herself, a difference whose foundation does not even necessarily have to do with clinical knowledge or skill, but with the therapist's role as an interacting human other. Therapists are, however, trained not only to be observant but to be particularly alert to alternative ways of understanding the client's presentation of himself or herself.

Mecke (1990) provided a list of fundamental characteristics of dialogue that sound very much like elements of good treatment:

1. The dialogic partners must engage with each other in good faith.
2. All possible norms and opinions must be open to potential questioning in the dialogic process.
3. Each participant must have the opportunity to be both speaker and hearer, with alternation between these roles.
4. The mark of dialogue is, above all, the interpenetration of different conceptions of the world. Here, of course, the client is presumed to have sought out a therapist *because* the therapist's view of the world is expected to be both different and useful. Thus the roles and areas of expertise of the two parties are quite different, with the client being knowledgeable about his or her own life experience and the therapist knowledgeable about more ways in which this experience can be understood.
5. The aim of all dialogue is consensus. Perhaps not all clinicians would initially agree with this way of conceiving of therapeutic dialogue. Yet it is in the areas where both client and therapist have worked hard to arrive at mutually satisfactory perspectives on the client's issues that we generally consider evidence of therapeutic effectiveness.

An additional characteristic on Mecke's (1990) list has particular significance for the present focus on the environment: dialogic participants must be able to incorporate the situation surrounding them into their exchange by making elements of it part of the theme of the conversation. Clearly, the situation surrounding the client and the therapist involves elements of the treatment room, the understanding of the client's problems and goals, and the understanding of the nature of the help that the psychotherapist has to offer (in the case of a clinic or agency, it will also involve the structure and purposes of the setting beyond the treatment room). However, the larger societal context, with its influences on the lives of both the client and the therapist as well as on the conduct of the treatment itself, also has to be included.

Bakhtin (1981) believed that elements of the environment are invariably a part of the dialogue, partly because language is social from its very beginning. Beyond this, however, Bakhtin argued that meaning is not in the words that are spoken; rather, meaning is realized only in the process of an active attempt at understanding. Meaning resides not in the word, but in the effect of the interaction between the speaker and the listener. The meaning of particular words cannot be understood outside the situation in which they are spoken.

There is, however, another sense in which dialogue is quite different from Freud's conception of therapeutic communication, which relied on the method of free association by the patient and subsequent interpretation by the therapist. Underlying free association and interpretation was an assumed transmission model of communication. The transmission model conceives of a message that is fully formulated in advance by the sender and that is then transmitted intact to the receiver. Yet the idea of communication as the intact transmission of a preformulated message is highly questionable. For example, the very point of the "gossip" (or "pass it down the line") games of childhood is a demonstration of the extent to which a simple statement becomes distorted when transmitted through a number of individuals.

Bakhtin (1981) pointed out that all communication, even monologue, has an audience, and therefore the content of all communication involves contributions from no fewer than two participants: the addressor and the addressee. There are three aspects to Bakhtin's description:

1. The first involves multiplicity of meaning—that is, even simple statements normally can be interpreted in more than one way by the listener.
2. The second aspect is that of context—that is, any statement or text will be interpreted differently according to its context, and certainly the context of the client and the therapist will be different. Thus invariably, on both sides of the therapist–client pair, what is said will be different from what is heard.
3. Since communication always involves at least two participants, the topic under discussion (in line with the multiplicity of meaning and the contextual influences on interpretation and response) is essentially negotiated. If, in the process of an interaction, the client

finds that the therapist is not responding to the content of the dialogue in the manner expected, the client usually will not break off the interaction but will shift the emphasis in order to engage the therapist. In similar fashion, if the client seems not to react to an "interpretation" in the desired manner, the therapist will ordinarily move to another perspective. Bahktin notes that communicative partners actually do interact in order to agree not only on what is to be said but also on what is not to be said. As therapists, we know that sometimes this agreement may occur without the conscious awareness of either party.

How would a model involving negotiation through a dialogic process account for therapeutic effectiveness? Loewald (1980b), who indicated that his approach to treatment was an interpersonal one, thought it was necessary for the therapist to relate to the patient as having made *just a little more* progress than he or she actually had in order to help that person grow. Presumably, if the treatment dialogue attributes slightly more ability than has been demonstrated by the patient, the patient will gradually grow into that ability. Certainly, it has long been observed by family therapists that people do tend to take on whatever aspects are attributed to them by significant others with whom they are in close interaction. In order to have an image of the client as having made a little more progress, however, the therapist must be able to create, in conjunction with the client and through the use of symbols, an understanding of his or her identity.

Referring to all types of psychological healing systems throughout all cultures, Kleinman (1988) concludes:

In summary . . . what is necessary for healing to occur is that both parties to the therapeutic transaction are committed to the shared symbolic order. What is important is that the patient has the opportunity to tell his story, experiences the therapist's witnessing of that account, believes the therapist's interpretation of his problems, and comes to use the same symbolic vehicles of interpretation to make sense of his situation. Because of his own need to believe and the rhetorical skills of the therapist to make key symbols relevant to the experience of the sufferer, the sick person becomes convinced that a transformation of his experience is possible and is in fact happening. (137)

EMPATHY

ALTHOUGH ALL SCHOOLS of psychotherapy have considered the therapist's positive regard for the patient to be important, Kohut (1984) and his followers brought it more directly into consideration as the principal means through which the treatment works. Nevertheless, defining empathy satisfactorily has been very difficult, even by its most vocal proponents. Reed (1984) pointed out that there has been so much confusion about empathy that it has been considered variously a process, a capacity, a form of knowledge, a form of communication, a means of understanding, a form of perceiving, an ability, and a mode of gathering data. Within this confusion, the notion of empathy has retained a sort of mystical overlay that then has extended to conceptualizations of the therapeutic process as a whole.

Orthodox psychoanalytic theory, conceptualizing affects as energic forces that were derivatives of the drives, seems to have postulated empathy almost as an energic field in which one could "resonate" with another's feelings (Easser 1974; Olden 1953). This approach made it seem as if being a good clinician required having highly refined "receptive capacities" with which to receive the affect signals of the client. There have been a number of problems with this approach, including that it has never been clear how to specify the manner in which these receptive capacities work or how they could be acquired.

Another approach to empathy, derived more from object relations theory, has been to assume that it relies on processes of psychological merger. Yet, from this perspective, it has been hard to know how to differentiate mergers that would lead to truly attuned empathy from pathological conditions that were presumed to develop from psychologically merged conditions. In this regard, Sanville (1991), relying on Bakhtin, has pointed out that pure merger would lead merely to a repetition of the inner experience of the other person. If this were all that occurred, then the clinician would simply replicate the experience of the client and would have no different perspective from which to be useful to the client. Thus therapeutic empathy must be conceptualized as something other than a simple merger.

While some theorists have seen empathy as involving a type of affect transfer, others, such as Buie (1984), have regarded it as more cognitively based. It does seem likely that different processes have been lumped together as empathy, but making distinctions on a strictly affective/cognitive basis, as has often been done (e.g., Lewis 1978), simply perpetuates the notion of a split between these two entities, which Bruner (1986) has referred to as having pernicious effects on clinical theory. In creating the notion of vitality affects as unconscious but nevertheless real interaction patterns that can be observed and on which empathy can be based, Stern (1985) seems to have made an important contribution. However, while empathy is based on affect attunement, Stern sees it has involving much more:

> Is attunement sufficiently close to what is generally meant by empathy? No. The evidence indicates that attunements occur largely out of awareness and almost automatically. Empathy, on the other hand, involves the mediation of cognitive processes. What is generally called empathy consists of at least four distinct and probably sequential processes: (1) the resonance of feeling state; (2) the abstraction of empathic knowledge from the experience of emotional resonance; (3) the integration of abstracted empathic knowledge into an empathic response; and (4) a transient role identification. (145)

The intrapsychic framework within which conceptions of empathy in psychotherapy have taken place, however, appears to have precluded the consideration of knowledge of the patient's environment as playing a part in empathy. Greenson perhaps came the closest to doing so. In his now classic paper on empathy, Greenson (1960) indicated that empathy requires an oscillation between the knower and the known. Greenson said that in treatment he built up in his mind a working model of what the patient was like, including everything he knew about the patient's history and customary reactions in the present. He then used this model to try to understand how the patient might feel about the circumstances that were currently being considered. For example, when a patient was describing an encounter that had taken place at a party, Greenson said he "went to the party as the patient." Notice here that Greenson said he had built up a working model of the patient, not that he built another model of the party. Yet being able to understand the patient and the patient's reactions at the party, he would also have needed cultural knowledge of what the kind of party his patient was likely to have attended would be like.

Knowledge of the party can, perhaps, be taken for granted if one assumes that it is simply a part of what Berger and Luckman (1966) referred to as "what everyone knows about a social world"—the common elements of the local culture. They do note, however, that this category includes "an assemblage of maxims, morals, proverbial nuggets of wisdom, values and beliefs, myths, and so forth, the integration of which requires considerable intellectual fortitude in itself, as the long line of heroic integrators from Homer to the latest sociological system-builders testifies" (65). Culture can be invisible in psychotherapy, but this is so only when therapist and client share a world view (Cavell 1993). In the current society of ever increasing diversity, psychothera-pists (and their patients) can no longer assume that they know "what everyone knows" about each other's worlds. This increasing diversity is already putting more pressure on therapists and theorists to recognize the cultural aspects of empathy and to find ways of dealing with this in the treatment, and it will continue to do so.

Two brief vignettes can help to illustrate the manner in which culture can enter into a therapist's ability to understand client communications.

Mrs. V. was a fifty-two-year-old woman in therapy for depression after the breakup of her third marriage. Having spent her childhood in the rural South, Mrs. V. had first married early in her adolescence as an attempt to escape her family's poverty and her sense of shame at her inability to compete with the "belles" from the better-off families that she envied. Each marriage had indeed improved her financial condi-tion, but she had experienced all three of her husbands as brutal men who, although willing to provide monetarily, had expected both sex and servitude on her part to be their due.

In the middle phase of treatment, Mrs. V. presented a dream in which one event was that of smoking as she walked along a street lined with stores. Knowing that, particularly at the time of Mrs. V.'s adoles-cence, a woman who smoked on the street in the South was considered a tramp, I called this image to Mrs. V.'s attention. Mrs. V.'s associations eventually led to an understanding of the major significance of both her identification with and her rebellion against her overburdened mother, whose frustrated ambitions had led her to transmit to her daughter a horror of being considered "white trash," but little in the way of assis-tance in learning how to function in social situations or to achieve a sense of personal self-esteem as a woman.*

---

*This case was initially presented and discussed in C. Saari, "Empathy in clinical social work: Playing in transcontextual space," *Journal of Analytic Social Work* 2 (1994): 25–42.

In the work with Mrs. V., I was able to use some cultural knowledge to help us increase our understanding. In the next example, however, the problem was a lack of such knowledge.

Mr. T., a middle-aged man, had an advanced degree from a prominent university. He was highly successful in his work, and his manner and appearance struck me as very upper middle class. Yet he described having grown up in a community of "hillbillies" who had little commerce with the mainstream culture. His father had allowed him and his nine siblings to attend school, but had forbidden the reading of any books other than the Bible in the home. The house in which he had lived had no running water, and he recalled bitterly the other children at school having made jokes about how dirty he and other hill children were.

I had serious difficulty imagining the Mr. T. I knew as having grown up under these conditions, and although I had no reason to believe that he was lying about or grossly exaggerating his background, I did sometimes wonder if the conditions he described really existed. Since this experience was clearly important to Mr. T.'s self-image, I decided to call a friend who lived in the general area and asked if there really were such people. The friend confirmed that indeed there were and recommended that I watch a documentary film that had been made about them. Doing so was enormously helpful in my being able to feel empathic with Mr. T.

Note that the clients in these examples were actually Caucasian Americans who participated in the "mainstream culture." Differences involving minority status or racial backgrounds between the members of therapist–client pairs greatly magnify the need for cultural knowledge. The issue is not that the therapist needs to know every detail of every possible background in order to carry out good therapy; rather, it is that the therapist needs to know the importance of such knowledge and be willing to be taught by the client and/or other sources.

As all postmodern theory holds, meaning cannot become decontexted, but Nelson (1985:27) notes that it can become *trans*contexted; that is, it can be moved from one context to another. Recall that the case in chapter 5 discussed Blanche's inability to have her own life be meaningful outside the context of her hometown (she could not transfer her identity and the meaning of her life to the culture of New York City). It is the ability to transcontext meaning that is required of the psychotherapist in being able to be empathic with clients. The therapist must have some ability to understand what the early environment the client describes might have brought out in a growing child. Conversely, the therapist must be able to wonder what kind of environment might have influenced a client to have the particular character traits he or she now has. To do so is not, of course, to discover some objective truth about the client's life, but to look for possible alternative ways of understanding the client's identity that might serve that person better in his or her current functioning.

Empathy in psychotherapy is not an achievement that, once reached, remains present in some intact form; rather it is a continual process that occurs throughout the treatment. In this regard, Knoblauch (1996) says: "I propose that mutative activity can be more usefully understood in terms of a sequence or stream of interactive moments co-constructed by analyst and analysand that configure an intersubjective field or context. . . . Any momentary action becomes meaningful only as it is framed by contextual expectations in a way that shapes its capacity to provide an analyst and/or analysand with insight, empathy, or a sense of authenticity" (322). This process requires the therapist to maintain, to the extent possible, conditions under which the creation of meaning can be favored, including the management of interpsychic space.

The maintenance of an empathic relationship within the treatment also requires that the therapist keep in mind a picture of who the client is and what that client's goals are. It is not possible to make a relationship with a *DSM* diagnosis. Relationships must be formed with individual human beings. Loewald (1980b), as mentioned earlier, thought that the analyst should relate to the patient as just a little more than he or she is at present. This is very much like Vygotsky's (1978) "zone of proximal distance," a concept developed in teaching young children. Vygotsky pointed out that there is a difference between the level at which a child can perform when working alone and the level at which the child can perform when working with an interacting but not directive adult, and he called that difference the zone of proximal distance. Teaching, Vygotsky thought, should be within that zone because the zone shows what the child is ready to learn next. In order, however, to achieve an image of the client as the client is at present, the therapist needs to construct a version of the client's identity.

Molly was a thirty-three-year-old separated woman when she first contacted me. She had seen a series of therapists, all of whom had refused to treat her after seeing her only once. She had recently made a serious suicide attempt, having taken enough medication for migraine headaches to land her in the hospital in a coma for three days. Following this, she had refused the recommended in-patient psychiatric treatment, saying that she needed only outpatient psychotherapy, and had signed herself out of the hospital against advice. The other therapists she had seen had refused to treat her unless she first signed herself into a hospital, which she refused to do. She could not, she claimed, afford to do this financially. She assured me that she was not suicidal; she had never really wanted to kill herself and so knew that she would not attempt suicide again. She seemed unaware that the details she provided of her impulsive attempt made it evident that such rashness was indeed likely to recur. A talk with her former therapist in another state nevertheless convinced me to try working with her.

Trying to get to know Molly was a difficult process, not because she was resistant but because the information she provided was so scattered. Almost fully immersed in the moment, Molly had a complicated history, and she offered pieces of it as they related to present concerns. But getting an integrated picture seemed impossible. Her life had involved a father who came from Southern aristocracy but who was an alcoholic and a gambler; a mother who came from a poor family and who had worked in a cotton mill; mental abuse from the father, who did things like forcing her to sleep with her nose pressed against the wall and then awakening her if this position had not been maintained; attending thirteen schools before she finished high school, with brief stays on both coasts and some places in between; a divorce between her parents when she was five years old; being shipped off to live with a grandparent when she was nearing adolescence; caretaking of younger siblings from an early age; being raped twice; two marriages, with a child from each; and drug abuse, including at one point heroin addiction. Trying to figure out even a chronology of all this, to say nothing of the details, was a daunting task.

At the time I began seeing Molly, I was only beginning to understand the value of narrative in psychotherapy. I knew, however, that for my own functioning I needed to put what I did know into some organized form, even if this should later turn out to be inaccurate. It took me considerable time to organize and write out Molly's history as I knew it then. What it did, of course, was to help me grasp the fact that Molly's life had been as scattered and as unpredictable as she seemed during the treatment hour. When I finished Molly's history, I began asking myself why I had needed to make this chronology—I knew it must be full of omissions and inaccuracies. Furthermore, I had told it from my perspective, which was undoubtedly not Molly's. I doubted that Molly was capable of putting her story together. In sessions, she usually gave me a detailed chronology of her life since she had seen me last. If I interrupted to comment or ask a question, she would usually say, "Wait, I am not finished yet." If she did finish before the hour was up, she would sit back and expect me to be able to tell her how she was, what all this meant.

In constructing Molly's story for myself, I had created a person to whom I could relate during our sessions, and having this narrative helped me feel much more comfortable in working with her. I wondered at the time I first wrote the narrative what Molly's reaction would be if I were to share it with her, but I did not think it likely to be useful to her. Molly's life continued to be full of chaos, with other impulsive suicide attempts; a seriously abusive man she dated; problems and guilt regarding the care of her children, who lived with her second husband; problems with drug abuse; and more. Molly, however, kept coming to see me, and slowly things got a little better for her in a process that I am now and was then at a loss to describe.

After a number of years of work with Molly, she became involved in a lawsuit, for which she wanted me to release a report on her treatment to her lawyer. I somewhat reluctantly agreed to do this, but only if she first read the record, including my (by then much amended) history, and knew what information about her it contained. She read it first in my office and had little reaction except to correct a few inaccuracies. She then took it home with her, read it again there, and by her account went to bed for a week. What hit her, she said, was how very mixed up this person was. Things have continued to get better, and, although I have little real evidence for it, I believe that reading my account of her life was ultimately useful to her in her attempts construct her own story of herself. She continues to have difficulties, but is far less impulsive and now has a stable marriage and a third child she enjoys caring for in a way she could not with her first two.

I provide the account of Molly's history not because I believe that there was anything unusually empathic about my work with her, other than perhaps a willingness to stick with her throughout the chaos. What I want to emphasize instead is the need that we psychotherapists have to create an identity for the patients we treat, and that this is a need shared by both therapist and client. The identity is not, of course, carved in stone, but has to be flexible and amendable as life proceeds. Cavell (1993) has said: "First, 'empathy' cannot be a matter of my getting somehow outside my own mind and into yours, but rests rather in discovering and widening the common base we share, exercising my imagination in regard to the beliefs and desires you may have in respect to which your behavior seems more or less reasonable to you" (34).

In a study dealing with how therapists working with children in therapeutic schools make decisions regarding what to do in the process of treatment sessions, Mann (1999) determined that what seems to occur is that the therapist creates a "narrative model of the case" and then uses it to think about the meaning of what is occurring in the session. Mann believes that the narrative form is important because it can integrate not only the information gained directly from the child, but also that which was obtained from others in the child's milieu, such as teachers or bus drivers—information that is critical to understand both the child and his or her environment. Narrative seems to be the form into which humans are naturally able to put their symbolizations. It is a form that is capable of including both the person and the environment and can, thereby, help both psychotherapists and clients to appreciate our identities.

CONCLUSION

THE CURRENT IMPACT of postmodernism on theories of psychotherapy has been primarily in understanding the relationship
between therapist and patient and in recognizing that the therapist
does not have access to a privileged truth. References to the importance
of context and culture are also now more frequent, but there continues
to be an underlying general assumption that culture is outside the treatment room. In spite of the emphasis on context in postmodernism, there
has been little consideration of the environment other than the setting in
which the treatment itself takes place. This lack of attention to the environment has been a problem for some time, although it was noticed by
relatively few theorists. Erikson (1975), however, noted:

> While it is true that no situation affords a better controlled access to
> the workings of the unconscious than does the psychoanalytic one,
> the greatest difficulty in the path of psychoanalysis as a general psy-
> chology probably consists in the remnants of its first conceptualiza-
> tion of the environment as an "outer world." To a patient under
> observation, the "world" he records (and, more often than not,
> complains about) easily becomes a hostile environment—"outer" as
> far as his most idiosyncratic wishes are concerned, and "outside" his
> precious relation to this therapist. This reveals much about him and
> about man; but it seems difficult to account for the nature of the
> clinical laboratory if the nature of the human environment is
> not included in the theory which guides the therapeutic encounter.
> (105)

The advent of postmodern theory, however, has made it possible
to create a theory in which the "inner" and the "outer" can be seen as
interrelated.

In this book, a number of important aspects of postmodern thought have been used to create the outlines of a theory of psychosocial functioning and psychotherapy. They include

- An appreciation of attachment and intersubjective perspectives on human relationships
- An understanding that affect and cognition are not split opposites, but form a unified process through which the person is connected to his or her environment and is able to evaluate the implications of that environment for the safety or danger of the self
- An understanding that not only is the nature of the person dynamic and constantly changing, but the environment, too, is constantly changing
- An awareness of the centrality of the process of meaning making in human functioning
- A recognition of the importance of a culture or shared meaning system that connects people to one another in communities and to the nonhuman environment as well
- An acceptance of a view of psychological health as involving a multiplicity or complexity of self as the person interrelates with different environments
- An understanding that meaning is not inherent in the human organism, but is created through the use of language
- A recognition that actions do not mask or distort inner meanings, but constitute the material from which meaning is created

Nelson's (1985, 1986, 1989) work has been particularly important in this regard because her theory provides five different ways in which psychological and linguistic development involve interrelationships with the sociocultural surround. Thus her theory allows for a perspective on person–environment configurations that involves more complexity than most other theories and therefore is able to capture more of the intricate manner in which the many aspects of human functioning are intertwined. First, Nelson tells us that children learn through social participation in their immediate environment. Children whose environments lack interaction with human others and/or stimulation from an inviting physical surround are at a disadvantage in life from its outset. Indeed, we now know that interaction with the environment is essential even for the development and functioning of the brain.

Second, children's knowledge of the world takes the form of event representations—that is, not accurate representations of separate and individual objects, but representations that involve an episodic unit of experience as a whole. Thus knowledge is never "true," or objective, but invariably evolves from the perspective of the individual and therefore always involves bias. It is on these event representations that the child forms a picture of what the world is like, an essential picture if the child is to be able to predict what is likely to happen in everyday activities and to be prepared to participate appropriately in these activities. The child's achievement of a picture of the world also enables an understanding of his or her place within that world. The child's understanding of the world, then, precedes and forms the basis for an identity—"who I am in the world." For better or worse, the individual's understanding of self includes that picture of the surrounding environment, and, as Loewald (1980a) noted, a loss of a sense of reality always means a loss of a sense of self. This remains true even if the surrounding reality seems to indicate a negative view of the self. Yet for some children whose lives involve much chaos in the immediate surround, it may even be difficult to create a stable system of event representations, and such an environment may therefore either prohibit or make very difficult the achievement of any sense of self at all.

Third, the child's introduction to language—the medium through which human beings can represent to themselves and to others their understanding of the world—takes place within the communal setting into which the child is born. Therefore language, and the thought it makes possible, is invariably social from its outset. Additionally, since the child's event representations are formed on the basis of social participation in the immediate environment, such knowledge is always cultural—always based on the practices sanctioned within the immediate caregiving group. New event representations and modifications to old ones continue to be formed throughout the lifespan, and ordinarily they seem to require social participation for their formation. Thus mere knowledge of different cultures or lifestyles acquired through passive means of learning, such as television or movies, does not usually enable an altered identity; however, adults do, ordinarily, have the possibility of using an internal dialogue between self and an external other or between different aspects of self.

Fourth, the ability to perform intrapersonal cognitive operations on information that has been acquired can be internalized only through the interpersonal sharing of perceptions of the external world. Vygotsky's

(1962, 1978) idea that all things occur twice, once in the external world and again in the internal world, is relevant here. The child's world is cultural both in the sense that social participation is required to enable potential representation and in the sense that, in order to be able to use these representations in communication with self or others, the child must contemplate or share the representations with a human other in order to acquire the ability to master their use. The child who has limited access to others who are interested in sharing that child's experience with the world will, therefore, be at a disadvantage for the development of affective/cognitive abilities. Poorly developed affective/cognitive abilities apply not only to the person's thoughts about the external world, but also to thoughts about the inner world. Thus the development of an inner life through which to consider options for behavior can be stunted as a result of a lack of interaction with others regarding the nature of the environment.

Finally, the words used in language are inherited from the broader linguistic community into which the child is born, and later in life the meanings of these words are negotiated within that larger community. It is through words, used to symbolize experiences with self and world, that the individual is able to arrive at new ideas and new ways of understanding his or her place in the world. If they are to have a lasting effect on the person's identity, potentially significant insights about the self based purely on a new combination of words must be considered within previously internalized representations of self, and then be integrated into these representations. Thus words are not enough, but under environmental conditions that foster the creation of meaning, words can be the beginning of a process of change.

PSYCHOTHERAPY INCLUDES MORE THAN INDIVIDUAL THERAPY

SERIOUS CONSIDERATION of the place of the environment in a theory for psychotherapy holds much more promise than what has been discussed in this book, which indeed has provided more of an outline for a theory than a fully formulated theoretical proposition. Thus the standard statement of "next questions" that is usually made at the end of a work such as this has much more than routine importance. There are, in fact, a multiplicity of directions for further thought. There are, however, two general arenas in which further understanding of the significance of the environment seems particularly promising, and the first of these would make possible a single theoretical base with which to encompass all the modalities currently employed in psychotherapeutic work.

The discussions of theory in this book have been focused on individual psychotherapy as the treatment modality, but this has been done at least partly for simplicity of presentation. In fact, the same theory can be used in the conduct of individual, couple, family, or group therapy. Although the treatment techniques used in these different types of therapy differ to accommodate the population and format involved, it ought to be possible to have a single, overall theory of therapeutic action. Of the case illustrations in this book, the Flynns, Pat, and Blanche dealt with issues in families; Martha and Estella involved couple therapy; and Blanche's case also involved participation in a group. A part of what is occurring theoretically is that postmodern theory is influencing the practice of all forms of therapy at the same time, and it thereby has potential for rendering obsolete the quarrels that practitioners have had with one another. Burch and Jenkins (1999), referring to the barriers that have separated psychoanalytic theory and family therapy into separate clinical domains, observed: "As relational theories have come to the forefront of psychoanalytic practice, the rationale for this rigid separation is fading. Family systems theories and relational psychodynamic theories all recognize the interdependence of individuals within a relational matrix; both rely upon a shift in one part of the system or matrix to stimulate responsive change to the other" (230).

It is probably in family therapy that the influence from postmodern approaches first was felt and now is most obvious. It has been in this area that Gergen's (1994; McNamee and Gergen 1992) social constructionism has had its greatest effect. Narrative theory and practice is now ubiquitous within family therapy (Wedge 1996; White and Epston 1990), and the discourse in family-therapy literature, rather than involving merely an initial observation of potential significance, now often includes a critical discussion of the utility of different aspects of postmodernism for family therapy. Lannamann (1998), in a particularly sophisticated example of this approach, argues that family therapy has become so heavily involved in seeing relationships as discourse that there has to be more recognition of people as embodied social beings.

Postmodernism also has had a significant impact on treatment of couples as a semi-autonomous aspect of family therapy. Johnson and Lebow (2000), in a review of current trends in couple therapy, note that postmodernism has had a major effect in many of the same ways it has affected family therapy, but interestingly they also note "a new interest in emotion as a positive, organizing force in human affairs and a vital part of individual and couple therapy" (32). Johnson and Lebow point out that the regulation of emotion is now generally recognized as a defining feature of close relationships; they comment that this has changed the tenor of couple therapy, making it less impersonal.

Current literature within group therapy appears to have been less influenced by postmodernism, but it does seem to be a compatible arena for such ideas, and their presence can be discerned. For example, Diamond (1996) says, "In this article I am not saying there is no 'inner' and no 'outer.' What I am saying is that the *relation between* them comes first, and makes possible the intercommunication between persons that characterizes human relationships and the creative work that takes place in the group setting [italics in original]" (314). The concept of culture, too, appears in group literature. Both Pfeifer (1992) and Spinner (1992) discuss the coexistence in children's therapy groups of indigenous peer culture and a therapeutic group culture. In commenting on a previous lack of attention to the group-as-a-whole in the literature, Schamess (1992) notes that behaviors that had been viewed as "provocative and unmanageable in traditionally conceptualized therapeutic groups" can now be seen as attempts to attach to a peer culture. He then notes:

> This formulation implicitly modifies how therapists view the treatment process. It conceptualizes treatment in interpersonal as well as intrapsychic terms, that is, as a series of interactions in which therapist and group members mutually influence each other on the basis of their past and present, real and internalized relationships. These relationships are enacted or reenacted on an individual basis in dyadic and triadic interactions and collectively in the ebb and flow of the evolving group-as-a-whole culture. (355)

Interestingly, it also seems that a postmodern approach may be enlivening discussions of milieu therapy, which has been very much neglected in the era of deinstitutionalization and managed care. An interesting, although perhaps not fully generalizable, transition can be seen in selected works in this field. Goffman's *Asylums*, in which the hospital patient was seen to be harmed through being held captive within a total institution, appeared in 1961. Weinstein's (1982) criticism of *Asylums*, although not attracting anything like the attention that Goffman's work did, argued that, while inpatient hospitalization no doubt did have its negative effects, patients also experienced the hospitalization as positive and needed to be responsible participants in the hospital's organizational life. In 1989, Swenson and Munich discussed the use of a large-group meeting in a therapeutic community as a way of helping patients understand the manner in which community-relevant events contribute to strains in the hospital. In 1994, Winer and Ornstein similarly discussed the use of community meetings in inpatient work, presenting this approach with the conscious use of postmodern ideas and the notion of "relational configurations" that bridge the intrapsychic and the interpersonal worlds. Thus there does appear to be a postmodern influence on milieu therapy.

Shapiro and Carr (1991), in a work discussing institutions and organizations that, while it does not note explicit awareness of postmodern ideas is certainly compatible with them, provide some concepts that may well also be useful in other modalities of therapy. First, they note that an institution or organization that forgets its task will invariably encounter difficulties—an observation that is related to, although not precisely the same as, the importance in psychotherapy of remaining consciously focused on the goal of the work. Second, they see the person's role as contingent on the task: when the focus is not on the task, role confusion develops. Finally, they stress the importance of ritual action as a starting place for reference and the creation of shared meaning among its participants.

Postmodern influences that seem appropriate to all modalities of psychotherapy also include several more themes: the significance of mirroring, not in Kohut's (1994) sense of selfobjects, but in Bakhtin's (1990) sense that because we cannot see how we appear to others, we need others in order to know ourselves; Mitchell and Black's (1995:79) emphasis on the present more than on the past and therefore a view of the therapist as a full participant in interpersonal patterns created within the therapy; and a fundamental recognition that psychotherapy does not reverse causes, but deals with the meanings of effects (Saari 1991).

SOCIAL OPPRESSION

THE SECOND GENERAL AREA in which further consideration of the role of the environment seems to hold promise is that of social oppression. Although Freud's theory dealt almost exclusively with phenomena that he thought of as intrapsychic, he did have hopes that psychoanalysis would make a major contribution to social problems (Altman 1995). Some theorists, particularly those of the Frankfurt school (Adorno, Fromm, Habermas, and Marcuse), attempted to combine psychoanalysis and sociological theory for a theory of social reform. Although this aspect of Freud's legacy has been more influential in Europe than in the United States, psychoanalytic theory may well still hold some promise for a theory of social reform.

Within the profession of social work, there have been many attempts to combine clinical work and social reform through seeing the goals of therapy to include empowerment. Foucault's theory, however, should warn us of the likelihood that the inclusion of social reform within psychotherapy has considerable potential to continue the oppression of the individual, although perhaps in another form, particularly since the goal of empowerment may well be that of the therapist rather than the client. Foucault does, however, remind us that even though great shifts in power distributions are rare, it is through individual subjectivity that resistance can be effective. As discussed in part 2, psychotherapy can contribute to clients' domination or liberation, and it may well be that a psychotherapy that aims to empower its clients would do best to concentrate on their goals for themselves and to have some confidence that, if individuals are empowered through some new freedom, they can then behave in ways that constitute Foucault's resistance. From a reformist perspective, the important thing would be to work toward making psychotherapy of excellent quality, available to the poor and oppressed— something that clearly does not now exist.

It has been emphasized here that psychotherapy appropriately deals not with causes, but with effects in the present. A theory and practice of social reform does need to have more of an emphasis on the elimination of causes; a theory of psychosocial functioning and psychotherapy that includes the environment within its domain, however, may well contribute to goals and methods that strengthen the efficacy of social interventions. At the very least, such a theory should reduce the hostility that sometimes shows itself between clinicians and social reformers. It may enable a more productive cooperation between them, and it is, of course, always possible that a more developed theory of the environment will point to as-yet-unconscious formulations of ways in which psychotherapy and social reform could work together for the benefit of all.

Stern (1997) has pointed out that

culture is not imposed from without; it is the fabric of our "within." Culture is not only responsible for our notions of the content and structure of the self; it is culture that determines whether the idea of a self is formulated at all.

In challenging us to see that every concept is a social product, social constructionism reveals that we have more choice about how we think than we generally believe we do. Since each set of ideas has implications for living and may influence the course of human lives, our awareness of the degree of choice operative in our intellectual life gives us a heightened sense of responsibility for how we think and what we believe. The complaint is sometimes made by opponents that social constructionism encourages relativism and moral chaos; a better argument is that it leads to a greater sense of social responsibility. (288–289)

Understanding the interrelated nature of inner and external worlds ought to lead to more useful ways of knowing both how to ensure better conditions for the development of human psychosocial functioning and how to improve the efficacy of psychotherapy.

REFERENCES

Adams, M. V. (1996). *The multicultural imagination: "Race," color, and the unconscious.* New York: Routledge.

Ainsworth, M. D. S., M. C. Blehar, E. Waters, and S. Wall (1978). *Patterns of attachment: A psychological study of the strange situation.* Hillsdale, N.J.: Erlbaum.

Altman, N. (1995). *The analyst in the inner city: Race, class, and culture through a psychoanalytic lens.* Hillside, N.J.: Analytic Press.

Amini, F., T. Lewis, R. Lannon, A. Louie, G. Baumbacher, T. McGuiness, and E. Z. Schiff (1996). Affect, attachment, memory: Contributions toward psychobiologic integration. *Psychiatry* 59: 213–240.

Applegate, J. S. (1999). Winnicott and the paradoxes of intersubjectivity. *Smith College Studies in Social Work* 69: 203–220.

Aron, L. (1996). *A meeting of minds: Mutuality in psychoanalysis.* Hillsdale, N.J.: Analytic Press.

Bakhtin, M. M. (1981). *The dialogic imagination.* Ed. M. Holquist. Austin: University of Texas Press.

Bakhtin, M. M. (1990). *Art and answerability: Early philosophical essays.* Ed. M. Holquist and V. Liapunov. Austin: University of Texas Press.

Basch, M. F. (1976). The concept of affect: A re-examination. *Journal of the American Psychoanalytic Association* 24: 759–777.

Basch, M. F. (1983). Empathic understanding: A review of the concept and some theoretical considerations. *Journal of the American Psychoanalytic Association* 31: 101–126.

Bass, E., and L. Davis (1988). *The courage to heal: A guide for women survivors of child sexual abuse.* New York: HarperCollins.

Bass, E., and L. Davis (1994). *The courage to heal: A guide for women survivors of child sexual abuse.* 3d ed. New York: HarperCollins.

Benjamin, J. (1988). *The bonds of love: Psychoanalysis, feminism, and the problem of domination.* New York: Pantheon Books.

Benjamin, J. (1998). *The shadow of the other: Intersubjectivity and gender in psychoanalysis.* New York: Routledge.

Benjamin, J. (1999). Recognition and destruction: An outline of intersubjectivity. In S. A. Mitchell and L. Aron, eds., *Relational psychoanalysis: The emergence of a tradition*, pp. 181–200. Hillsdale, N.J.: Analytic Press.

Berger, P. L., and T. Luckmann (1966). *The social construction of reality: A treatise in the sociology of knowledge.* New York: Anchor Books.

Biestek, F. J. (1994). An analysis of the casework relationship. *Chicago: Families in Society,* 630–634.

Bion, W. R. (1962). *Learning from experience.* New York: Basic Books.

Blatt, S. J. (1974). Levels of object representation in anaclitic and introjective depression. *Psychoanalytic Study of the Child* 29: 107–157.

Bleuler, E. (1924). *Textbook of psychiatry.* New York: Macmillan.

Bolger, K. E., C. J. Patterson, W. W. Thompson, and J. B. Kupersmidt (1995). Psychosocial adjustment among children experiencing persistent and intermittent family economic hardship. *Child Development* 66: 1107–1129.

Bowlby, J. (1969). *Attachment and loss.* Vol. 1, *Attachment.* New York: Basic Books.

Bromberg, P. M. (1996). Standing in the spaces: The multiplicity of self and the psychoanalytic relationship. *Contemporary Psychoanalysis* 32: 509–535.

Bromberg, P. M. (1998). *Standing in the spaces: Essays on clinical process, trauma, and dissociation.* Hillsdale, N.J.: Analytic Press.

Bronfenbrenner, U. (1979). *The ecology of human development: Experiments by nature and design.* Cambridge, Mass.: Harvard University Press.

Brooks-Gunn, J., G. J. Duncan, and N. Maritato (1997). Poor families, poor outcomes: The well-being of children and youth. In G. J. Duncan and J. Brooks-Gunn, eds., *Consequences of growing up poor.* New York: Sage.

Bruner, J. (1986). *Actual minds, possible worlds.* Cambridge, Mass.: Harvard University Press.

Bruner, J. (1990). *Acts of meaning.* Cambridge, Mass.: Harvard University Press.

Bruner, J., and J. Lucariello (1989). Monologue as narrative recreation of the world. In K. Nelson, ed., *Narratives from the crib.* Cambridge, Mass.: Harvard University Press.

Buie, D. (1984). Discussion of Theodore Shapiro's "Empathy: A critical reevaluation." In J. Lichtenberg, M. Bornstein, and D. Silver, eds., *Empathy I*, pp. 129–136. Hillsdale, N.J.: Analytic Press.

Burch, B., and C. Jenkins (1999). The interactive potential between individual therapy and couple therapy: An intersubjective paradigm. *Contemporary Psychoanalysis* 35: 229–252.

Burchinal, M. R., F. A. Campbell, D. M. Bryant, B. H. Wasik, and C. T. Ramey (1997). Early intervention and mediating processes in cognitive performance of children of low-income African-American families. *Child Development* 68: 935–954.

Burman, E. (1994). *Deconstructing developmental psychology*. New York: Routledge.

Butler, J. (1990). *Gender trouble*. New York: Routledge.

Cavell, M. (1993). *The psychoanalytic mind: From Freud to philosophy*. Cambridge, Mass.: Harvard University Press.

Chambon, A. S., A. Irving, and L. Epstein, eds. (1999). *Reading Foucault for social work*. New York: Columbia University Press.

Corcoran, M., and T. Adams (1997). Race, sex, and the intergenerational transmission of poverty. In G. J. Duncan and J. Brooks-Gunn, eds., *Consequences of growing up poor*, pp. 461–517. New York: Sage.

Davies, J. M. (1996). Linking the "pre-analytic" with the postclassical: Integration, dissociation, and the multiplicity of unconscious process. *Contemporary Psychoanalysis* 10: 552–577.

Demos, E. V. (1982). Affect in early infancy. *Psychoanalytic Inquiry* 1: 533–575.

Diamond, N. (1996) Can we speak of internal and external reality? *Group Analysis* 29: 303–317.

Dooley, J. W. (1998). Negotiating identities in life decisions: Life stories of gay men. Ph.D. diss., Loyola University Chicago.

Dorpat, T. L. (1996). *Gaslighting: The double whammy, interrogation, and other methods of covert control in psychotherapy and analysis*. Northvale, N.J.: Aronson.

Duncan, G. J., and J. Brooks-Gunn, eds. (1997). *Consequences of growing up poor*. New York: Sage.

Easser, R. (1974). Empathic inhibition and psychoanalytic technique. *Psychoanalytic Quarterly* 43: 557–580.

Elliott, R., and L. S. Greenberg (1997). Multiple voices in process-experiential therapy: Dialogues between aspects of the self. *Journal of Psychotherapy Integration* 7: 225–239.

Emde, R. N. (1989). The infant's relationship experience: Developmental and affective aspects. In A. J. Sameroff and R. N. Emde, eds., *Relationship disturbances in early childhood: A developmental approach*, pp. 33–52. New York: Basic Books.

Emde, R. N. (1992). Social referencing research: Uncertainty, self, and the search for meaning. In S. Feinman, ed., *Social referencing and the social construction of reality in infancy*, pp. 79–94. New York: Plenum.

Erikson, E. H. (1958). *Young man Luther*. New York: Norton.

Erikson, E. H. (1962). Reality and actuality. *Journal of the American Psychoanalytic Association* 10: 451–474.

Erikson, E. H. (1963). *Childhood and society.* 2d ed. New York: Norton.

Erikson, E. H. (1964). *Insight and responsibility*. New York: Norton.

Erikson, E. H. (1969). *Gandhi's truth*. New York: Norton.

Erikson, E. H. (1975). *Life history and the historical moment: Diverse presentations*. New York: Norton.

Fast, I. (1998). *Selving: A relational theory of self organization*. Hillsdale, N.J.: Analytic Press.

Feinman, S. (1992). In the broad valley: An integrative look at social referencing. In S. Feinman, ed., *Social referencing and the social construction of reality in infancy*, pp. 3–13. New York: Plenum.

Feinman, S., D. Roberts, K. Hsieh, D. Sawyer, and D. Swanson (1992). A critical review of social referencing in infancy. In S. Feinman, ed., *Social referencing and the social construction of reality in infancy*, pp. 15–54. New York: Plenum.

Fennell, G. (1998). Indicators of identity complexity as identified in a client journal. Ph.D. diss., Loyola University Chicago.

Fish, B. (1996). Clinical implications of attachment narratives. *Clinical Social Work Journal* 24: 239–253.

Flax, J. (1990). *Thinking fragments: Psychoanalysis, feminism, and postmodernism in the contemporary West*. Berkeley: University of California Press.

Flax, J. (1996). Taking multiplicity seriously: Some implications for psychoanalytic theorizing and practice. *Contemporary Psychoanalysis* 32: 577–593.

Fonagy, P. (1999). Transgenerational consistencies of attachment: A new theory. Paper delivered to the Developmental and Psychoanalytic Discussion Group, American Psychoanalytic Association meeting, Washington, D.C., May 13.

Fonagy, P., M. Target, M. Steele, and H. Steele (1997). The development of violence and crime as it relates to security of attachment. In J. D. Osofsky, ed., *Children in a violent society*, pp. 150–177. New York: Guilford Press.

Foucault, M. (1962). *Mental illness and psychology*. Berkeley: University of California Press.

Foucault, M. (1988). *Madness and civilization: A history of insanity in the age of reason.* New York: Vintage Books.

Foucault, M. (1990). *The history of sexuality: An introduction.* Vol. 1. New York: Vintage Books.

Foucault, M. (1995). *Discipline and punish: The birth of the prison.* 2d ed. Ed. and trans. A. Sheridan. New York: Vintage Press.

Freud, S. (1915/1955). The unconscious. In *The standard edition of the complete psychological works of Sigmund Freud,* vol. 14, pp. 166–204. London: Hogarth Press.

Freud, S. (1920/1957). Beyond the pleasure principle. In *The standard edition of the complete psychological works of Sigmund Freud,* vol. 18, pp. 7–64. London: Hogarth Press.

Freud, S. (1923/1961). The ego and the id. In *The standard edition of the complete psychological works of Sigmund Freud,* vol. 19, pp. 3–66. London: Hogarth Press.

Friedman, R. J., and J. M. Natterson (1999). Enactments: An intersubjective perspective. *Psychoanalytic Quarterly* 68: 220–247.

Geller, J. D. (1998). What does it mean to practice psychotherapy scientifically? *Psychoanalysis and Psychotherapy* 15: 187–214.

Gergen, K. J. (1994). *Realities and relationships: Soundings in social construction.* Cambridge, Mass.: Harvard University Press.

Goffman, E. (1962). *Asylums: Essays on the social situation of mental patients and other inmates.* Chicago: Aldine.

Goldberg, L. (1997). A psychoanalytic look at recovered memories, therapists, cult leaders, and undue influence. *Clinical Social Work Journal* 25: 71–86.

Goldstein, E. (1994). Self-disclosure in treatment: What the therapists do and don't talk about. *Clinical Social Work Journal* 22: 417–433.

Greenberg, J. A., and S. A. Mitchell (1983). *Object relations in psychoanalytic theory.* Cambridge, Mass.: Harvard University Press.

Greenson, R. R. (1960). Empathy and its vicissitudes. *International Journal of Psychoanalysis* 41: 418–424.

Grotstein, J. S. (1994). Foreword to *Affect regulation and the origin of the self: The neurobiology of emotional development,* by A. N. Schore, pp. xxi–xxviii. Hillsdale, N.J.: Erlbaum.

Groves, B. M., and B. Zuckerman (1997). Intervention with parents and caregivers of children who are exposed to violence. In J. D. Osofsky, ed., *Children in a violent society,* pp. 183–201. New York: Guilford Press.

Guidano, V. F. (1987). *The complexity of the self: A developmental guide to psychopathology and therapy*. New York: Guilford Press.

Hamilton, C. E. (2000). Continuity and discontinuity of attachment from infancy through adolescence. *Child Development* 71: 690–694.

Harrell, S. P. (2000). A multidimensional conceptualization of racism-related stress: Implications for the well-being of people of color. *American Journal of Orthopsychiatry* 70: 42–57.

Harris, A. (1996). The conceptual power of multiplicity. *Contemporary Psychoanalysis* 32: 537–552.

Hartman, A. (1988). Foreword to *Paradigms of clinical social work*, ed. R. A. Dorfman, pp. vii–xi. New York: Bruner/Mazel.

Hartmann, H. (1958). *Ego psychology and the problem of adaptation*. Trans. D. Rapapport. New York: International Universities Press.

Hartwell, C. E. (1996). The schizophrenogenic mother concept in American psychiatry. *Psychiatry* 59: 274–297.

Hernandez, D. J. (1997). Poverty trends. In G. J. Duncan and J. Brooks-Gunn, eds., *Consequences of growing up poor*, pp. 18–34. New York: Sage.

Hirsch, I. (1996). Observing-participation, mutual enactment, and the new classical models. *Contemporary Psychoanalysis* 32: 359–383.

Hoffman, I. Z. (1998). *Ritual and spontaneity in psychoanalytic process: A dialectical-constructivist view*. Hillsdale, N.J.: Analytic Press.

Holma, J., and J. Aaltonen (1995). The self-narrative and acute psychosis. *Contemporary Family Therapy* 17: 307–316.

Hudson, J., L. R. Shapiro, and B. B. Sosa (1995). Planning in the real world: Preschool children's scripts and plans for familiar events. *Child Development* 66: 984–998.

Hudson, J. A., and E. G. Sheffield (1998). Déjà vu all over again: Effects of reenactment on toddlers' event memory. *Child Development* 69: 51–67.

Izard, C. E. (1971). *The face of emotion*. New York: Appleton-Century-Crofts.

Jacobson, E. (1964). *The self and the object world*. New York: International Universities Press.

Johnson, S., and J. Lebow (2000). The "coming of age" of couple therapy: A decade review. *Journal of Marital and Family Therapy* 26: 23–38.

Kernberg, O. F. (1990). New perspectives in psychoanalytic affect theory. In R. Plutchik and H. Kellerman, eds., *Emotion: Theory, research, and experience*, vol. 5, pp. 115–131. New York: Academic Press.

Klein, G. S. (1976). Freud's two theories of sexuality. In *Psychoanalytic theory*, pp. 72–120. New York: International Universities Press.

Kleinman, A. (1988). *Rethinking psychiatry: From cultural category to personal experience*. New York: Free Press.

Kohut, H. (1984). *How does analysis cure?* Chicago: University of Chicago Press.

Krause, I. (1998). *Therapy across cultures*. London: Sage.

Krystal, H. (1988). *Integration and self-healing: Affect, trauma, and alexithymia*. New York: Analytic Press.

Kuebli, J., and R. Fivush (1994). Children's representation and recall of event alternatives. *Journal of Experimental Child Psychology* 58: 25–45.

Lachmann, F. M. (1996). How many selves make a person? *Contemporary Psychoanalysis* 32: 595–614.

Lakoff, G. (1987). *Women, fire, and dangerous things: What categories reveal about the mind*. Chicago: University of Chicago Press.

Lane, R. D., and G. E. Schwartz (1987). Levels of emotional awareness: A cognitive-developmental theory and its application to psychopathology. *American Journal of Psychiatry* 144: 133–143.

Lannamann, J. W. (1998). Social construction and materiality: The limits of indeterminacy in therapeutic settings. *Family Process* 37: 393–423.

Lewis, J. M. (1978). *To be a therapist*. New York: Bruner/Mazel.

Lichtenstein, H. (1977). *The dilemma of human identity*. New York: Aronson.

Loewald, H. W. (1980a). Ego and reality. In *Papers on psychoanalysis*, pp. 3–20. New Haven, Conn.: Yale University Press.

Loewald, H. W. (1980b). On the therapeutic action of psychoanalysis. In *Papers on psychoanalysis*, pp. 221–256. New Haven, Conn.: Yale University Press.

Loewald, H. W. (1980c). Primary process, secondary process, and language. In *Papers on psychoanalysis*, pp. 178–206. New Haven, Conn.: Yale University Press.

Loewald, H. W. (1980d). Psychoanalysis as an art and the fantasy character of the psychoanalytic situation. In *Papers on psychoanalysis*, pp. 352–371. New Haven, Conn.: Yale University Press.

Loewald, H. W. (1980e). The experience of time. In *Papers on psychoanalysis*, pp. 138–147. New Haven, Conn.: Yale University Press.

Lomas, P. (1990). *The limits of interpretation*. Northvale, N.J.: Aronson.

Lorenzer, A., and P. Orban (1978). Transitional objects and transitional phenomena: Socialization and symbolization. In S. A. Grolnick, L.

Barkin, and W. Munsterberger, eds., *Between reality and fantasy: Winnicott's concepts of transitional objects and phenomena.* Northvale, N.J.: Aronson.

Lucariello, J., A. Kyratzis, and K. Nelson (1992). Taxonomic knowledge: What kind and when? *Child Development* 63: 978–998.

Lucariello, J., and K. Nelson (1985). Slot-filler categories as memory organizers for young children. *Developmental Psychology* 21: 272–282.

Lucariello, J., and A. Rifkin (1986). Event representations as the basis for categorical knowledge. In K. Nelson, ed., *Event knowledge: Structure and function in development,* pp. 189–204. Hillsdale, N.J.: Erlbaum.

Mahler, M. S., F. Pine, and A. Bergman (1975). *The psychological birth of the human infant.* New York: Basic Books.

Main, M., and H. Morgan (1996). Disorganization and disorientation in infant strange situation behavior. In L. K. Michaelson and W. J. Ray, eds., *Handbook of dissociation: Theoretical, empirical, and clinical perspectives.,* pp. 107–138. New York: Plenum.

Mandler, J. M. (1984). *Stories, scripts, and scenes: Aspects of schema theory.* Hillsdale, N.J.: Erlbaum.

Mann, K. A. (1999). Reflective school social work practice: An exploration of clinical decision making with youths identified as seriously emotionally disturbed. Ph.D. diss., Loyola University Chicago.

Maranhao, T. (1990). Introduction to *The interpretation of dialogue,* ed. T. Maranhao, pp. 1–24. Chicago: University of Chicago Press.

McLoyd, V. C. (1998). Socioeconomic disadvantage and child development. *American Psychologist* 53: 185–204.

McNamee, S., and K. J. Gergen, eds. (1992). *Therapy as social construction.* Newbury Park, Calif.: Sage.

Mead, G. H. (1934). *Mind, self, and society.* Ed. C. Morris. Chicago: University of Chicago Press.

Meche, J. (1990). Dialogue in narration (the narrative principle). In T. Maranhao, ed., *The interpretation of dialogue,* pp. 195–215. Chicago: University of Chicago Press.

Mitchell, S. A. (1988). *Relational concepts in psychoanalysis: An integration.* Cambridge, Mass.: Harvard University Press.

Mitchell, S. A. (1993). *Hope and dread in psychoanalysis.* Cambridge, Mass.: Harvard University Press.

Mitchell, S. A. (1998). The analyst's knowledge and authority. *Psychoanalytic Quarterly* 68: 1–31.

Mitchell, S. A., and L. Aron, eds. (1999). *Relational analysis: The emergence of a tradition*. Hillsdale, N.J.: Analytic Press.

Mitchell, S. A., and M. J. Black (1995). *Freud and beyond: A history of modern psychoanalytic thought*. New York: Basic Books.

Modell, A. H. (1990). *Other times, other realities: Toward a theory of psychoanalytic treatment*. Cambridge, Mass.: Harvard University Press.

Moore, R. (1999). *The creation of reality in psychoanalysis: A view of the contributions of Donald Spence, Roy Schafer, Robert Stolorow, Irwin Z. Hoffman, and beyond*. Hillsdale, N.J.: Analytic Press.

Morris, P., ed. (1998). *The Bakhtin reader: Selected writings of Bakhtin, Medvedev, Voloshinov*. London: Arnold.

Morson, G. S., and C. Emerson (1990). *Michael Bakhtin: Creation of a prosaics*. Stanford, Calif.: Stanford University Press.

Murachver, T., M. Pipe, R. Gordon, J. L. Owens, and R. Fivush (1996). Do, show, and tell: Children's event memories acquired through direct experience, observation, and stories. *Child Development* 67: 3029–3044.

Nathanson, D. L. (1992). *Shame and pride: Affect, sex, and the birth of the self*. New York: Norton.

Nelson, K. (1985). *Making sense: Development of meaning in early childhood*. New York: Academic Press.

Nelson, K. (1986). *Event knowledge: Structure and function in development*. Hillsdale, N.J.: Erlbaum.

Nelson, K. (1988). The ontogeny of memory for real events. In U. Neisser and E. Winograd, eds., *Remembering reconsidered: Ecological and traditional approaches to the study of memory*. New York: Cambridge University Press.

Nelson, K. (1989). *Monologues from the crib*. Cambridge, Mass.: Harvard University Press.

Nemiah, J. C., and P. E. Sifneos (1970). Psychosomatic illness: A problem in communication. *Psychotherapy and Psychosomatics* 18: 154–160.

O'Brien, C. (1999). Contested territories: Sexualities and social work. In A. S. Chambon, A. Irving, and L. Epstein, eds., *Reading Foucault for social work*, pp. 131–155. New York: Columbia University Press.

Ogden, T. H. (1994). The analytic third: Working with intersubjective clinical facts. *International Journal of Psychoanalysis* 75: 3–19.

Olden, C. (1953). On adult empathy with children. *Psychoanalytic Study of the Child* 8: 111–126.

Parton, N. (1999). Reconfiguring child welfare practices: Risk, advanced liberalism, and the government of freedom. In A. S. Chambon, A. Irving, and L. Epstein, eds., *Reading Foucault for social work*, pp. 101–130. New York: Columbia University Press.

Perlman, H. H. (1979). *Relationship: The heart of helping people*. Chicago: University of Chicago Press.

Pfeifer, G. (1992). Complementary cultures in children's psychotherapy groups: Conflict, coexistence, and convergence in group development. *International Journal of Group Psychotherapy* 42: 357–368.

Piaget, J. (1962). *Play, dreams, and imitation in childhood*. New York: Norton.

Pizer, S. A. (1996). The distributed self: Introduction to symposium on "The multiplicity of self and analytic technique." *Contemporary Psychoanalysis* 32: 499–507.

Polkinghorne, D. E. (1988). *Narrative knowing and the human sciences*. Albany: State University of New York Press.

Raines, J. C. (1996). Self-disclosure in clinical social work. *Clinical Social Work Journal* 24: 357–375.

Reed, G. S. (1984). The antithetical meaning of empathy in psychoanalytic discourse. In J. Lichtenberg, M. Bornstein, and D. Silver, eds., *Empathy I*, pp. 7–24. Hillsdale, N.J.: Analytic Press.

Renik, O. (1993). Analytic interaction: Conceptualizing technique in the light of the analyst's irreducible subjectivity. *Psychoanalytic Quarterly* 62: 553–571.

Renik, O. (1997). Reactions to "Observing-participation, mutual enactment, and the new classical models," by Irwin Hirsch. *Contemporary Psychoanalysis* 33: 279–285.

Robbins, F. P., and L. A. Sadow (1974). A developmental hypothesis of reality processing. *Journal of the American Psychoanalytic Association* 22: 344–363.

Rollock, D., and E. W. Gordon (2000). Racism and mental health into the 21st century: Perspectives and parameters. *American Journal of Orthopsychiatry* 70: 5–13.

Rubin, S. S. (1997). Self and object in the postmodern world. *Psychotherapy* 34: 1–10.

Saari, C. (1986). *Clinical social work treatment: How does it work?* New York: Gardner Press.

Saari, C. (1988). Interpretation: Event or process? *Clinical Social Work Journal* 16: 378–389.

Saari, C. (1991). *The creation of meaning in clinical social work*. New York: Guilford Press.

Saari, C. (1993). Identity complexity as an indicator of health. *Clinical Social Work Journal* 21: 11–24.

Saari, C. (1994). Empathy in clinical social work: Playing in transcontextual space. *Journal of Analytic Social Work* 2: 25–42.

Saari, C. (1998). Intersubjectivity, language, and culture: Bridging the person/environment gap? *Smith College Studies in Social Work* 69: 203–220.

Saari, C. (2001). Counteracting the effects of invisibilty in work with lesbian clients. *Journal of Clinical Psychology: In Session* 57: 645–654.

Saleebey, D. (1992). *The strengths perspective in social work practice*. New York: Longman.

Sands, R. G. (1996). The elusiveness of identity in social work practice with women: A postmodern perspective. *Clinical Social Work Journal* 24: 167–186.

Sanville, J. (1991). *The playground of psychoanalytic therapy*. Hillsdale, N.J.: Analytic Press.

Saussure, F. de (1959). *Course in general linguistics*. New York: Philosophical Library.

Schafer, R. (1980). Narration in the psychoanalytic dialogue. *Critical Inquiry* 7: 29–53.

Schafer, R. (1983). *The analytic attitude*. New York: Basic Books.

Schafer, R. (1992). *Retelling a life*. New York: Basic Books.

Schafer, R. (1997). *Tradition and change in psychoanalysis*. Madison, Conn.: International Universities Press.

Schamess, G. (1992). Reflections on a developing body of group-as-a-whole theory for children's groups: An introduction. *International Journal of Group Psychotherapy* 42: 351–356.

Schank, R., and R. Abelson (1977). *Scripts, plans, goals, and understanding*. Hillsdale, N.J.: Erlbaum.

Schimek, J. G. (1975). A critical reexamination of Freud's concept of unconscious mental representation. *International Review of Psychoanalysis* 2: 171–187.

Schooler, C. (1999). The workplace environment: Measurement, psychological effects, and basic issues. In S. L. Friedman and T. D. Wachs, eds., *Measuring environment across the life span: Emerging methods and concepts*, pp. 229–246. Washington, D.C.: American Psychological Association.

Schore, A. N. (1994). *Affect regulation and the origin of the self: The neu-robiology of emotional development*. Hillside, N.J.: Erlbaum.

Searles, H. F. (1960). *The non-human environment*. New York: International Universities Press.

Seidman, S. (1998). *Contested knowledge: Social theory in the postmodern era*. 2d ed. Malden, Mass.: Blackwell.

Seidman, S., K. Nelson, and J. Gruendel (1986). Make believe scripts: The transformation of ERs in fantasy. In K. Nelson, ed., *Event knowledge: Structure and function in development*, pp. 161–187. Hillsdale, N.J.: Erlbaum.

Seton, P. H. (1981). Affect and issues of separation-individuation. *Smith College Studies in Social Work* 52: 1–11.

Shapiro, E. R., and A. W. Carr (1993). *Lost in familiar places: Creating new connections between the individual and society*. New Haven, Conn.: Yale University Press.

Shapiro, J. R., and J. S. Applegate (2000). Cognitive neuroscience, neurobiology, and affect regulation: Implications for clinical social work. *Clinical Social Work Journal* 28: 9–21.

Shawver, L. (1996). What postmodernism can do for psychoanalysis. *American Journal of Psychoanalysis* 56: 371–394.

Shweder, R. A. (1990). Cultural psychology: What is it? In J. W. Stigler, A. Richard, and G. Herdt, eds., *Cultural psychology: Essays on comparative human development*, pp. 1–43. Cambridge: Cambridge University Press.

Siegel, D. J. (1999). *The developing mind: Toward a neurobiology of interpersonal experience*. New York: Guilford Press.

Slavin, M. O. (1996). Is one self enough? Multiplicity in self-organization and the capacity to negotiate relational conflict. *Contemporary Psychoanalysis* 32: 615–625.

Spinner, D. A. (1992). The evolution of culture and cohesion in the group treatment of ego impaired children. *International Journal of Group Psychotherapy* 42: 369–380.

Spitz, R. A. (1965). *The first year of life: A psychoanalytic study of normal and deviant development of object relations*. New York: International Universities Press.

Stern, D. B. (1992). Commentary on constructivism in clinical psychoanalysis. *Psychoanalytic Dialogues* 2: 331–363.

Stern, D. B. (1997). *Unformulated experience: From dissociation to imagination in psychoanalysis*. Hillsdale, N.J.: Analytic Press.

Stern, D. N. (1985). *The interpersonal world of the infant*. New York: Basic Books.

Stevens, J. W. (1996). Childbearing among unwed African-American adolescents: A critique of theory. *Affilia* 11: 278–302.

Stolorow R. D., and G. E. Atwood (1992). *Contexts of being: The intersubjective foundations of psychological life.* Hillsdale, N.J.: Analytic Press.

Sullivan, H. S. (1953). *The interpersonal theory of psychiatry: Collected works.* Vol. 1. New York: Norton.

Susko, M. A. (1994). Caseness and narrative: Contrasting approaches to people who are psychiatrically labeled. *Journal of Mind and Behavior* 15: 87–112.

Swenson, C. R., and R. L. Munich (1989). Types of large-group meetings in the therapeutic community. *Psychiatry* 52: 437–445.

Tessler, M., and K. Nelson (1994). Making memories: The influence of joint encoding on later recall by young children. *Consciousness and Cognition* 3: 307–326.

Tolpin, M. (1971). On the beginnings of a cohesive self. *Psychoanalytic Study of the Child* 26: 316–352.

Tomkins, S. S. (1962). *Affect/imagery/consciousness.* Vol. 1, *The positive affects.* New York: Springer.

Trevarthen, C., and P. Hubley (1978). Secondary intersubjectivity: Confidence, confiders, and acts of meaning in the first year. In A. Lock, ed., *Action, gesture, and symbol.* New York: Academic Press.

Voloshinov, V. N. (1973). *Marxism and the philosophy of language.* Trans. L. Matejka and I. R. Tutunik. New York: Seminar.

Von Bertalanffy, L. (1968). *General system theory: Foundations, development, applications.* New York: Braziller.

Vygotsky, L. S. (1962). *Thought and language.* Cambridge, Mass.: MIT Press.

Vygotsky, L. S. (1978). *Mind in society: The development of higher psychological processes.* Cambridge, Mass.: Harvard University Press.

Wang, F. T. Y. (1999). Resistance and old age: The subject behind the American seniors movement. In A. S. Chambon, A. Irving, and L. Epstein, eds., *Reading Foucault for social work*, pp. 189–217. New York: Columbia University Press.

Waters, E., C. E. Hamilton, and N. S. Weinfield (2000). The stability of attachment security from infancy to adolescence and early adulthood: General introduction. *Child Development* 71: 678–683.

Waters, E., S. Merrick, D. Treboux, J. Crowell, and L. Albersheim (2000). Attachment security in infancy and early adulthood: A twenty-year longitudinal study. *Child Development* 71: 684–689.

Wedge, M. (1996). *In the therapist's mirror: Reality in the making*. New York: Norton.

Weinfield, N. S., L. A. Sroufe, and B. Egeland (2000). Attachment from infancy to early adulthood in a high-risk sample: Continuity, discontinuity, and their correlates. *Child Development* 71: 695–702.

Weinstein, R. M. (1982). Goffman's *Asylums* and the social situation of mental patients. *Orthomolecular Psychiatry* 11: 267–274.

Werner, H., and B. Kaplan (1963). *Symbol formation*. New York: Wiley.

Wertsch, J. V. (1985). *Vygotsky and the social formation of the higher psychological processes*. Cambridge, Mass.: Harvard University Press.

White, M., and D. Epston (1990). *Narrative means to therapeutic ends*. New York: Norton.

Wiley, A. R., A. J. Rose, L. K. Burger, and P. J. Miller (1998). Constructing autonomous selves through narrative practices: A comparative study of working-class and middle-class families. *Child Development* 69: 833–847.

Winer, J. A., and E. Ornstein (1994). Relational themes in the inpatient community meeting. *International Journal of Group Psychotherapy* 44: 313–332.

Winnicott, D. W. (1958). *Collected papers: Through paediatrics to psychoanalysis*. New York: Basic Books.

Winnicott, D. W. (1965a). Ego distortion in terms of true and false self. In *Maturational processes and the facilitating environment*, pp. 140–152. New York: International Universities Press.

Winnicott, D. W. (1965b). *Maturational processes and the facilitating environment*. Madison, Conn.: International Universities Press.

Winnicott, D. W. (1971a). *Playing and reality*. London: Tavistock.

Winnicott, D. W. (1971b). The use of an object and relating through identifications. In *Playing and reality*, pp. 86–94. London: Tavistock.

Winnicott, D. W. (1975a). Hate in the countertransference. In *Through paediatrics to psychoanalysis*, pp. 194–203. New York: Basic Books.

Winnicott, D. W. (1975b). Transitional objects and transitional phenomenon. In *Through paediatrics to psychoanalysis*, pp. 229–242. New York: Basic Books.

Winnicott, D. W. (1986). *Holding and interpretation: Fragment of an analysis*. New York: Hogarth Press.

Zetzel, E. (1970). *The capacity for emotional growth*. Madison, Conn.: International Universities Press.

AUTHOR INDEX